A GUIDE TO
FORMING ARTS

THE HISTORY OF

# WESTERN DANCE

EDITED BY
TRENTON HAMILTON

**Britannica®**
Educational Publishing
IN ASSOCIATION WITH

# ROSEN
EDUCATIONAL SERVICES

Published in 2016 by Britannica Educational Publishing (a trademark of Encyclopædia Britannica, Inc.) in association with The Rosen Publishing Group, Inc. 29 East 21st Street, New York, NY 10010

Distributed exclusively by Rosen Publishing.
To see additional Britannica Educational Publishing titles, go to rosenpublishing.com.

First Edition

**Britannica Educational Publishing**
J.E. Luebering: Director, Core Reference Group
Anthony L. Green: Editor, Compton's by Britannica

**Rosen Publishing**
Hope Lourie Killcoyne: Executive Editor
Kathy Kuhtz Campbell: Senior Editor
Nelson Sá: Art Director
Brian Garvey: Designer
Cindy Reiman: Photography Manager
Introduction and supplementary material by Trenton Hamilton

### Library of Congress Cataloging-in-Publication Data

The history of Western dance/edited by Trenton Hamilton.
pages cm.—(The Britannica guide to the visual and performing arts)
Includes bibliographical references and index.
ISBN 978-1-68048-079-5 (library bound)
1. Dance—History—Juvenile literature. I. Hamilton, Trenton.
GV1596.5.H57 2016
793.309—dc23

2014042143

*Manufactured in the United States of America*

# CONTENTS

## CHAPTER 3
## THE 20TH AND 21ST CENTURIES      75

It is the wedding of movement to music. From soaring ballet leaps to the simple swaying at a high school prom. It is dance, a means of recreation, of communication—for the purpose of expressing an idea or emotion, releasing energy, or simply taking delight in the movement itself. Dance is perhaps the oldest, yet the most incompletely preserved, of the arts. Its origins are lost in prehistoric times, but, from the study of the most primitive peoples, it is known that men and women have always danced.

There are many kinds of dance. It can be a popular craze, like the moonwalk, the trademark dance of the "king of pop" Michael Jackson, or ballets that featured superstar performers such as David Hallberg and Natalia Osipova. It can be folk dances that have been handed down through generations, such as the square dance, or ethnic dances that are primarily associated with a particular country. It can be modern dance or musical comedy dancing, both fields

In the American Ballet Theatre's performance of *Giselle*, Natalia Osipova, as Giselle, and David Hallberg, as Count Albrecht, dance a pas de deux (a dance for two people).

that were pioneered by American men and women. Within the chapters of this book, the rich history of dance is chronicled from its early forms in ancient Egypt to the contemporary street dance styles of New York City.

Dances in primitive cultures all had as their subject matter the changes experienced by people throughout their lives, changes that occurred as people grew from childhood to old age, those they experienced as the seasons moved from winter to summer and back again, changes that came about as tribes won their wars or suffered defeats.

Two sorts of dance evolved as cultures developed: social dances on occasions that celebrated births, commemorated deaths, and marked special events in between; and magical or religious dances to ask the gods to end a famine, to provide rain, or to cure the sick. The medicine men of primitive cultures, whose powers to invoke the assistance of a god were feared and respected, are considered by many to be the first choreographers, or composers of formal dances.

Originally rhythmic sound accompaniment was provided by the dancers themselves. Eventually a separate rhythmic accompaniment evolved, probably played on animal skins stretched over wooden frames and made into drums or similar instruments. Later, melodies were added; these might have imitated birdcalls or other sounds of nature, or they might have been a vocal expression of the dancers' or musicians' state of mind. The rhythmic beat, however, was the most important element. This pulsation let all the dancers keep time together, and it helped them to remember their movements, too. By controlling the rhythm, the leader of a communal dance could regulate the pace of the movement.

Primitive dancers also shared certain gestures and movements, which were drawn from their everyday lives. People planting seeds swing their arms with unvarying regularity. People who are hungry rub a hand on their empty bellies. People who want to show respect or admiration bend down or bow before another individual. These gestures, and others like them, were part of the earliest dances.

There is also a large vocabulary of gestures that originated as a means of expressing bodily needs. Caresses are universally taken to signify tender feelings. Clenched fists mean anger. Hopping up and down indicates excitement. Primitive dancers used all of these movements in both their social and religious or magical dances. These dances were not created and performed for entertainment, as many dances are today. One of the major reasons for them was to help tribes survive. Long before the written word could guarantee that traditions would be passed on and respected, it was dance that helped the tribe preserve its continuity.

During the Renaissance, dance became popular at court. It became an essential part of every courtier's education to be able to dance and move gracefully. In England dancing was so popular among all classes that foreign ambassadors spoke of the people as the "dancing English."

During the 17th century the Puritans were rather effective at stamping out the most exuberant and pagan of English dance customs, although among the upper classes it was still considered proper for young children to learn to dance, as philosopher John Locke put it, to instill "a becoming confidence" in them. In America, the hold of the Puritans was even stronger, and many leaders frowned upon any kind of dance, recreational or otherwise, as idle and lascivious. Others saw it as a necessary part of education, as long as it was sober and serious. Gradually, dance as a means of physical education and entertainment became more popular in the United States. Folk dancing and social dancing were encouraged. Ballroom dancing and fashionable dances such as the minuet, quadrille, polka, and waltz—all of them originating in Europe—became popular by the mid-1800s.

None of these dances grew more popular than the waltz, which was first introduced to the Austrian court in the 17th century. Its gliding, whirling movements immediately became the rage throughout the entire population. Some people, however, found waltzing undignified, and in 1760 the performance of waltzes was banned by the church in parts of Germany. Nevertheless, the mania continued, and by the late 18th century waltzing was common in the cosmopolitan cities of London, England, and Paris, France. People felt the same spirit in the dance that they perceived in the great political events of the day—the French and the American revolutions.

The waltz stood for freedom of expression and freedom of movement. Unlike more courtly dances, with their restricted steps and predetermined poses, the waltz allowed the performers to sweep around the dance floor, setting their own boundaries and responsible to nobody but their partners.

By the early 20th century the waltz as an art form was exhausted. It found a final admirer in the French composer Maurice Ravel, whose orchestral piece *The Waltz* both celebrates the dance's traditions and mourns its passing out of fashion.

Around the time of World War I (1914–18), when America's attention was fixed on other lands around the globe, a dance craze developed that had strong international influence. From South America came the tango and the maxixe. European dances inspired the American couple Irene and Vernon Castle to develop many new sophisticated dances that won vast popularity and that were performed nationwide.

As the 20th century evolved, African and Caribbean rhythms and movements increasingly influenced social dancing. Swing, the jitterbug, the twist, boogie, and disco dancing all share a free and improvised movement style and a repetitive, percussive rhythm that can be traced to more primitive sources.

Another important influence was felt from Ireland, whose clog dances were first brought to America in the 1840s. After being adapted by local performers, clog dance steps became the tap dances done by generations of minstrels and music hall performers. Tap dancing was originally performed as an accompaniment to song. With costume, makeup, and scenery, it was another of the entertainer's accessories, its percussive and rhythmic patterns heightening a song's effectiveness.

Modern dancers, however, made tap an art form of its own. Rhythms grew more intricate, and movements became larger. Greater emphasis was placed on elements of dance composition and design, and greater value was shown to the music made by the taps themselves. Among the greatest tap dance artists are Bill "Bojangles" Robinson, who refined the minstrel tradition, and Fred Astaire, whose performances are unsurpassed for their musicality and grace.

Folk dancing preserved its own identity as these popular dances developed. By folk dance is meant a dance that originated in a particular country or locality and has become closely identified with its nation of origin. The czardas, for example, is unmistakably Hungarian, and the hora is linked to Israel. These dances are often performed by dedicated groups of amateurs who want either to preserve the dance tradition of their ancestors or to share in another country's culture.

Certainly in the Western world, dance as an art form has never been as popular as it is today, with a wide range of choreographic styles and genres attracting large audiences. As a form of recreation it has also undergone a massive revival, as can be seen in the resurgence of interest in swing and ballroom dancing and in the urban dance styles of contemporary music videos. Moreover, many folk dances, nearly lost to a broader public in the 20th century, have been carefully revived and are widely enjoyed; Irish dancing, Balkan dancing, and English country dancing were but a few of the popular participatory dances evident at the turn of the 21st century. In Asia and Africa many traditional dances have been transferred from the community, where they were dying out, to the theatre. This has brought about a rapid growth in their popularity, both in their places of origin and in the West, where they attract large audiences and are also studied.

The peoples of the West—of Europe and of the countries founded through permanent European settlement elsewhere—have a history of dance characterized by great diversity and rapid change. Whereas most dancers of the East repeated highly refined forms of movement that had remained virtually unchanged for centuries or millennia, Western dancers showed a constant readiness, even eagerness, to accept new vehicles for their dancing. From the earliest records, it appears that Western dance has always embraced an enormous variety of communal or ritual dances, of social dances enjoyed by many different levels of society, and of skilled theatrical dances that followed distinct but often overlapping lines of development. However, the West cannot always be clearly distinguished from the non-West, especially in such countries as Russia or other regions of the former Soviet Union, where some dances are Asian and others European in origin and character.

In this far-reaching study, readers reflect on a multitude of dance types, dance elements, such as movement, steps, rhythm, music, and costumes, and diverse dance traditions throughout the ages. This volume also spotlights the immeasurable talents of John Weaver, Augusta Maywood, Jean-Georges Noverre, Michel Fokine, Anna Pavlova, Vaslav Nijinsky, George Balanchine, Isadora Duncan, Agnes de Mille, Mary Wigman, Martha Graham, Jerome Robbins, Merce Cunningham, Twyla Tharp, and Savion Glover, among others, and their contributions to dance as a performing art.

# CHAPTER ONE

# DANCE AS AN ART FORM: FROM ANTIQUITY THROUGH THE RENAISSANCE

**B**efore written records were left, a vast span of time elapsed about which scholars can only speculate. Pictorial records in cave paintings in Spain and France showing dancelike formations have led to the conjecture that religious rites and attempts to influence events through sympathetic magic were central motivations of prehistoric dance. Such speculations have been reinforced by observation of dances of primitive peoples in the contemporary world, though the connection between ancient and modern "primitives" is by no means accepted by many scholars. If the dances recorded in early written records represented a continuity from prehistoric dances, there may have been prehistoric work dances, war dances, and erotic couple and group dances as well. One couple dance surviving in the 21st century, the Bavarian-Austrian *Schuhplattler*, is considered by historians to be of Neolithic origin, from before 3000 BCE.

# DANCE IN THE ANCIENT WORLD

In the civilizations of Egypt, Greece, and its neighbouring islands, and Rome, written records supplement the many pictorial remains. Written records alone provide information about ancient Jewish dancing. Even though there are still conjectures about the style, pattern, and purpose of ancient dances, the combination of pictorial and written evidence gives scholars a more concrete sense of what dance was like in ancient Egypt, Greece, and Rome, than these written-only records for Jewish dancing.

## ANCIENT EGYPTIAN DANCE

The first great culture to infuse its entire society with the magic of dance was that of Egypt. Far more than mere pastime, dancing became an integral part of Egyptian life. It evolved from the simplest rituals used by hunters to find their prey. Performing the dances was believed to help in later hunts. A leader, called a priest–dancer, was responsible for seeing that the dances were performed correctly so that the hunt would be successful.

Eventually these dances were separated from their ritual and became an art of their own. This development paralleled the emergence of Osiris as the Egyptians' most important god.

A detail from a wall painting in the tomb of Nebamun from Shaykh 'Abd al-Qurnah in Thebes, Egypt, depicts Egyptian dancers during a banquet, from around 1400 BCE.

With his mythical sister and wife, Isis, he was a symbol of a more developed civilization on Earth, and belief in him guaranteed everlasting life. Dance was a crucial element in the festivals held for Isis and Osiris. These occurred throughout the year—in the summer, for instance, when the Nile River began to rise and the corn was ripening, and in the fall on All Souls' Night—the ancient ancestor of Halloween. Dance was also important in the festivals dedicated to Apis, the bull associated with fertility rituals, and also in a ceremony in which priests portrayed the stars in celebration of the cosmos, or harmonious universe.

As was true in more primitive cultures, music was a part of these celebrations but not as important as the dancing itself. Egyptians had developed stringed, wind, and percussion instruments as well as different sorts of whistles and harps.

Dance figured, too, in private life. Professional performers entertained at social events, and traveling troupes gave performances in public squares of great cities such as Thebes and Alexandria.

Movements of Egyptian dances were named after the motion they imitated. For instance, there were "the leading along of an animal," "the taking of gold," and "the successful capture of the boat." Probably many of the poses and motions were highly acrobatic, though in certain instances Egyptian dance steps look remarkably like steps in classical ballet.

From Egypt also come the earliest written documentations of the dance. These records speak of a class of professional dancers, originally imported from the interior of Africa, to satisfy the wealthy and powerful during hours of leisure and to perform at religious and funerary celebrations. These dancers were considered highly valuable

possessions, especially the Pygmy dancers
who became famous for their artistry. One of
the pharaohs prayed to become a "dance
dwarf of god" after his death, and King Nefer-
kare (3rd millennium BCE) admonished one
of his marshals to rush such a "dance dwarf
from the Land of Spirits" to his court.

There is considerable agreement that
the belly dance, now performed by dancers
from the Middle East, is of African origin. A
report of the 4th century BCE from Memphis in
Egypt described in detail the performance of
an apparently rumba-like couple dance with
an unquestionably erotic character. The Egyptians also knew acrobatic exhibition dances
akin to the present-day adagio dances. They
definitely were aware of the sensual allure of
the sparsely clad body in graceful movement.
A tomb painting from Shaykh 'Abd al-Qurnah,
now in the British Museum, shows dancers
dressed only in rings and belts, apparently
designed to heighten the appeal of their
nudity. These figures probably were intended
to entertain the dead as they had been entertained in life.

Egypt, then, presented a dancing scene
that was already varied and sophisticated. In
addition to their own danced temple rituals
and the Pygmy dancers imported from the
headwaters of the Nile, there were Hindu dancing girls from conquered countries to the east.
Their dances had none of the long masculine

strides or the stiff, angular postures seen in so many Egyptian stone reliefs. Lines of movement undulated softly, nowhere bending sharply or breaking. These Asiatic girls brought a true feminine style to Egyptian dance.

## DANCE IN CLASSICAL GREECE

Many Egyptian influences can be found in the Greek dance. Some came by way of Crete, others through the Greek philosophers who went to Egypt to study. The philosopher Plato (c. 428–348/47 BCE) was among them, and he became an influential dance theoretician. He distinguished dances that enhance the beauty of the body from awkward movements that imitate the convulsions of ugliness. The Apis cult dances of Egypt had their equivalent in the Cretan bull dance of about 1400 BCE. It inspired the labyrinthine dances that, according to legends, Theseus brought to Athens on his return with the liberated youths and maidens.

Another dance form that originated in Crete and flourished in Greece was the *pyrrhichē*, a weapon dance. Practiced in Sparta as part of military training, it was a basis for the claim of the philosopher Socrates that the best dancer is also the best warrior. Other choral dances that came to Athens from Crete include two dedicated to Apollo and one in which naked boys simulated wrestling matches. Female characteristics were stressed

This terra-cotta sculpture of a Greek dancer exemplifies the beautiful movements that established Greece's theatrical form, from its beginnings in the Dionysian cult and rituals to its later dramatic art forms.

in a stately and devout round dance in honour of the gods, performed by choruses of virgins.

Numerous vase paintings and sculptural reliefs offer proof of an ecstatic dance connected with the cult of Dionysus. It was celebrated with a "sacred madness" at the time of the autumnal grape harvest. In his drama *Bacchae* (also called *Bacchants*), Euripides (c. 480–406 BCE) described the frenzy of Greek women, called bacchantes or maenads. In their dance for generation and regeneration, they frantically stamped the ground and whirled about in rhythmic convulsions. Such dances were manifestations of demoniacal possession characteristic of many primitive dances.

The Dionysian cult brought about Greek drama. After the women danced, the men followed in the disguise of lecherous satyrs. Gradually the priest, singing of the life, death, and return of Dionysus while his acolytes represented his words in dance and mime, became an actor. The scope of the dance slowly widened to incorporate subjects and heroes taken from the Homeric legends. A second actor and a chorus were added. In the lyric interludes between plays, dancers re-created the dramatic themes in movements adopted from the earlier ritual and bacchic dances. In the comedies, they danced the very popular *kordax*, a mask dance of uninhibited lasciviousness. In the tragedies, the chorus performed the *emmeleia*, a dignified dance with flute accompaniment.

These dances and plays were executed by skilled amateurs. At the end of the 5th century BCE, however, there came into being a special class of show dancers, acrobats, and jugglers, the female members of which were evidently *hetairai*, members of a class of courtesans. No doubt influenced by Egyptian examples, they entertained guests at lavish banquets. The historian Xenophon (c. 430–c. 355 BCE) in his *Symposium* tells of the praise Socrates lavished on a female dancer and a dancing boy at one such occasion, finally himself emulating their beautiful movements. Elsewhere, Xenophon describes a dance representing the union of the legendary heroine Ariadne with Dionysus, an early example of narrative dance.

According to the philosopher Aristotle (384–322 BCE), Greek tragedy originated in the myth of Dionysus's birth. He relates that the poet Arion was responsible for establishing the basic theatrical form, one that incorporated dance, music, spoken words, and costumes. There was always a chief dancer who was the leader of these presentations. As the form evolved, the leader became something close to what would now be considered a combination choreographer and performer, while other participants assumed the role of an audience. By the 6th century BCE, the basic form of theater as known today was established.

No matter how far Greek theatre moved from its original ritual sources, it was always connected with the myths of Dionysus. Participation in dance and drama festivals was a religious exercise, not merely an amusement. In Greek plays dance was of major importance, and the three greatest dramatists of the era—Aeschylus, Sophocles, and Euripides—were familiar with dance in both theory and practice. Sophocles, for example, studied both music and dance as a child, and, after the defeat of the Persians in the 5th century BCE, he danced in the triumphal celebration. In his childhood, Euripides had been affiliated with a troupe of dancers, and in plays such as *Bacchae*, his last great work, a dancing choir plays a role of major importance.

Even in earlier times dancing was popular among the Greek people. It was thought to promote physical health and to influence one's education positively. These attitudes were passed on from generation to generation. For instance, in Homer's epics, which date from the 11th to 10th century BCE, dance is portrayed as a kind of social pastime, not as an activity associated with religious observances. By the end of the 4th century BCE, dancing had become a professional activity. Dances were performed by groups, and the motion of most dances was circular. In tragic dances—where mimed expression, or wordless action, was important—the dancers would not touch one another. Generally, in fact, Greek dances were not based on the relationship between men and women. Most were performed by either one sex or the other.

Greek dance can be divided into large and small motions—movements and gestures. Movements were closely related to gymnastic exercises; schoolchildren had to master series of harmonious physical exercises that resembled dance. Gestures imitated poses and postures found in everyday life and conveyed all the emotions ranging from anger to joy. For musical accompaniment the Greeks used stringed instruments such as the lyre, flutes such as the panpipe, and a wide variety of percussion instruments, including tambourines, cymbals, and castanets.

Altogether there were more than 200 Greek dances designed for every mood and purpose. There were comic pieces, warlike works, and dances for athletes, spectacles, and religious worship. For purely social purposes there were dances for weddings, funerals, and seasonal celebrations connected with harvesttime. Yet these dances were not as important as those connected with the theatre. By the 5th century BCE, dancing had become recognized as an art.

## ANCIENT ROMAN DANCE

As early as 364 BCE entertainers from Greece were imported to Rome to perform theatrical pieces in honour of the gods and to amuse a population weary from a plague. These performers inspired the local population to develop plays of their own—mimes and bawdy farces that included elements of dance.

Roman culture, which eclipsed the Greek in approximately the 3rd century BCE, was in many ways influenced by Grecian models. In dance, however, the Romans distorted the balance and harmony that characterized the Greeks, putting the greatest emphasis on spectacle and mime. Dancing itself almost disappeared.

Roman theatre had originated in 240 BCE, when public games were held after the victory in the first Punic Wars. As part of these celebrations comedy and tragedy were performed, including drama, music, and dance. According to the writer Plutarch, dance included three elements: motion, posture, and indication, the last a gesture that pointed out some object near the performer.

Performances such as these fed the Romans' love of spectacle. Their desire to see a bustling stage full of people led to performances that took place in ever-larger spaces. Conventional theatres were replaced by the circus and the arena. To get his meaning across to such a large audience, a performer's gestures had to become cruder and coarser. Eventually the artist's skill was blunted, and with this loss of craftsmanship came a loss of social prestige. Dancers, who were honoured and respected by the Greeks, became little more than slaves to the Romans.

Though spectacles provided the Roman population with most of its dancing, social and domestic dances were also performed to a limited extent. Most of these had a religious or ritualistic nature. They prophesied events or appeased the gods. Dances were also designed for entertainment, with battle pieces the most common.

In general, however, dancing was not highly thought of. The famous orator Cicero said in a speech that "no man, one may almost say, ever dances when sober, unless perhaps he be a madman; nor in solitude, nor in a moderate and sober party; dancing is the last companion of prolonged feasting, of luxurious situation, and of many refinements."

As the Roman Empire expanded, secular dances showed exotic influences. People from Africa to Britain fell under Roman rule, but their strange, foreign movements and gestures were never truly integrated into a style of dance the Romans could call their own. Like the artworks among their plunder, the dances were merely novelties and curiosities.

A form of dance that enjoyed great popularity with the Romans under the emperor Augustus (63 BCE–14 CE) was the wordless, spectacular pantomime that rendered dramatic stories by means of stylized gestures. The performers, known as *pantomimi*, were at first considered more or less as interpreters of a foreign language, since they came from Greece. They refined their art until the two dancer-mimes Bathyllus and Pylades became the star performers of Augustan Rome. The stylized performance of the dancer, who wore a mask appropriate to the theme of his dance, was accompanied by musicians playing flutes, horns, and percussion instruments and a chorus that sang about the action between dance episodes. According to the writings of the 2nd-century Greek satirist Lucian of Samosata, Roman pantomime was a highly developed art form that made lavish and creative use of dance. Though the Romans showed little use for the dance as developed by the Greeks, they excelled in this new form of pantomime dance–drama.

## JEWISH DANCE

When dance is mentioned in the Hebrew Bible it is distinguished by its joyousness. Words such as leaping and whirling describe the energy and vitality of ancient Hebrew dances. As in other early societies, dancing is most often connected with ritualistic activity.

Ring dances may have been performed in the worship of the golden calf; the prohibition against making graven images that resulted from this worship explains the lack of evidence of Jewish dances in the visual arts.

Hebrew dances were performed by both men and women, though usually the sexes were separated. Victory dances were performed by groups of women; men participated in ecstatic whirling dances designed to evoke prophecy. Festival dances were performed by both groups—one of the most important was the water-drawing festival on the first night of the holiday of Sukkoth, which was celebrated by a torch-lit procession dance that lasted through the night.

Weddings provided another important occasion for ritual dancing. Dancing with the bride was considered an act of devotion, and the officiating rabbi always complied with pleasure. During the Diaspora of the early Christian era many of the ritual dances disappeared, but the bridal dance continued as a tradition. In the Middle Ages wedding dances were performed in which men danced with the bridegroom and women with the bride because of the segregation of the sexes. Later, men could dance with the bride either by wrapping their hands in a cloth or by holding a cloth between them to signify their separation.

# CHRISTIANITY AND THE MIDDLE AGES

Dancing was traditional also among the tribes of barbarians to the north, as attested by the writings of the Christian missionaries. Wherever they went, they found the same fertility-rite dances—if in different guise, the same charm dances to induce good and ward off evil, the same warrior and weapon dances to bolster fighting morale, and the same uncontrolled expressions of the joy of life, which the missionaries attributed to the devil.

Erotic dancing was not the exclusive property of heathen societies. In Byzantium, the Christian emperor Justinian I (483–565) married the notorious Theodora, a dancer who had appeared in the nude in theatrical performances. About 500, St. Caesarius of Arles reported a sacrificial banquet ending in some demoniacal dancing rites performed to the accompaniment of lewd songs. The Anglo-Saxons had little girls performing dances at Easter in which a phallus was carried in front of them.

## ECCLESIASTICAL ATTITUDES AND PRACTICES

The attitude of the Christian Church toward dance was not unanimous. On the one side there was the ascetic rejection of all manifestations of lust and ecstasy, and dance was seen as one of the strongest persuasions to sexual permissiveness. On the other side, some early Church Fathers tried to find functions for pagan dances in Christian worship. St. Basil of Caesarea in 350 called dancing the noblest activity of the angels, a theory later endorsed by the Italian poet Dante. St. Augustine (354–430) was strictly against dancing, but, despite his great influence in the medieval church, dancing in churches continued for centuries.

Charlemagne, the Holy Roman emperor at the beginning of the 9th century, officially prohibited all kinds of dancing, but the ban was not observed. The Teutonic (Germanic) peoples were accustomed to dancing as part of their religious rites. On Christian feast days, which coincided with their ancient rites of expelling the winter, of celebrating the arrival of spring, and of rejoicing that the days grew longer again, they revived their old ritual dances, though these were camouflaged with new names and executed to different purpose. In this manner previously sacred dances became more and more secularized. After such secularization, two lines of development were open: the social dance or the assimilation of dance into theatrical spectacle by the joculators, travelling comedians who combined the arts of dancer, juggler, acrobat, singer, actor, mime, and musician in one person.

# THE DANCE OF DEATH

The dance of death, also known as danse macabre, was a medieval allegorical concept of the all-conquering and equalizing power of death, expressed in the drama, poetry, music, and visual arts of western Europe mainly in the late Middle Ages. Strictly speaking, it is a literary or pictorial representation of a procession or dance of both living and dead figures, the living arranged in order of their rank, from pope and emperor to child, clerk, and hermit, and the dead leading them to the grave. The dance of death had its origins in late 13th- or early 14th-century poems that combined the essential ideas of the inevitability and the impartiality of death. The concept probably gained momentum in the late Middle Ages as a result of the obsession with death inspired by an epidemic of the Black Death, a bubonic plague, in the mid-14th century and the devastation of the Hundred Years' War (1337–1453) between France and England. The mime dance and the morality play undoubtedly contributed to the development of its form.

The dance of death frequently appears in friezes decorating the cloisters of monasteries (the open courtyards of which usually contained cemeteries) and the naves of churches. There are also numerous German woodcut versions. German artist Hans Holbein, the Younger's depiction of the subject (1523-26) was perhaps the culminating point in the pictorial evolution of the dance of death. Holbein's drawings were then turned into woodcuts by Hans Lützelburger and published at Lyon in 1538. Holbein's procession is divided into separate scenes depicting the skeletal figure of death surprising his victims in the midst of their daily lives. Apart from a few isolated mural paintings in northern Italy, the theme did not become popular south of the Alps.

Before the Middle Ages, dance movements were part of the Latin Mass rites, along with music and dramatic dialogue. But by the Middle Ages, these works moved from inside the churches to the outside. On cathedral porches, church squares, and marketplaces, miracle plays, mystery plays, and morality plays that taught the church's lessons were enacted in a theatrical way. Rather than being part of the mass ritual, however, these pieces had become a form of entertainment.

Dance was also observed in two other sorts of activity. In dramatic ritual games with dance

movement the passing of the seasons was celebrated, even as it had been by primitive tribes;
and in the works of troubadours and other wandering minstrels, dance and song were used to
express the full range of human emotions.

## DANCE ECSTASIES

There were two kinds of dance peculiar to
the Middle Ages, the dance of death and the
dancing mania known as St. Vitus's dance. Both
originally were ecstatic mass dances, dating
from the 11th and 12th centuries. People congre-
gated at churchyards to sing and dance while
the representatives of the church tried in vain to
stop them. In the 14th century another form of
the dance of death emerged in Germany, the
*Totentanz*, a danced drama with the character
of Death seizing people one after the other without distinctions of class or privilege. The German
painter Hans Holbein the Younger (1497/98–
1543) made a famous series of woodcuts of
this dance.

The St. Vitus's dance became a real public
menace, seizing hundreds of people, spreading
from city to city, mainly in the Low Countries, in
Germany, and in Italy during the 14th and 15th
centuries. It was a kind of mass hysteria, a wild
leaping dance in which the people screamed
and foamed with fury, with the appearance of
persons possessed. In these convulsive, frantic,
and jerky dances, religious, medical, and social

"The Peddler," from Hans Holbein the Younger's series *Dance of Death* (*Totentanz;* 1523-26), shows Death stopping a peddler on the road and pulling him away from his destination.

influences probably interacted in response to such things as the epilepsy-like seizures of persons suffering from the Black Death. Italy was afflicted with tarantism, an epidemic presumably caused by the bite of venomous spiders. Its effects had to be counteracted by distributing the poison over the whole body and "sweating it out," which was accomplished by dancing to a special kind of music, the tarantella.

## DANCE AND SOCIAL CLASS

In western Europe by the 12th century, society had developed into three classes, the nobility, the peasantry, and the clergy. This separation contributed to the development of the social dance. The knights created their own worldly and spiritual ideals, exemplified in tournaments and courtly entertainments that were praised in song and poetry by the troubadours and minnesingers (German poet-musicians). The

In Pieter Bruegel the Elder's painting *The Wedding Dance* (detail; c. 1566), the artist shows colourful peasants dancing and making merry at a wedding celebration.

couple dances of the knights expressed the polished and aristocratic notions of courtly love. The round dances of the peasants were executed by circles or lines of people, often singing and holding each other by their hands. The rustic choral round had strong pantomimic leanings and unpolished expressions of joy and passion. And while the choral rounds almost always were executed to the singing of the participants, the court dances of the knights generally were accompanied by instrumental playing, especially of fiddles, and when there was singing, it emerged from the spectators rather than the performers.

From the late Middle Ages, graphic artists frequently recorded what dancing looked like in all its different manifestations. How dancing adapted to the idealism of knightly love is shown in manuscript illuminations and tapestries. Paintings of the Flemish painter Pieter Bruegel the Elder (c. 1525/30–69) leave no doubt that the peasants enjoyed celebrating with dances of uninhibited stamping and cavorting.

# THE RENAISSANCE WORLD AND THE ART DANCE

France had set the fashion in court dance during the late Middle Ages; with the Renaissance, however, Italy became the centre of the new developments in dance. The Renaissance brought greater mixing of social classes, new fortunes and personal wealth, and greater indulgence in worldly pleasures and in the appreciation of the human body. The period emerged as one of the most dance-conscious ages in history.

## COURT DANCES AND SPECTACLES

Celebrations and festivities proliferated. The itinerant jugglers of the Middle Ages became highly respected and much sought after as dancing masters. They quickly assumed the function of instructing the nobility not only in the steps but also on posture, bearing, and etiquette. They became responsible for the planning and realization of the spectacular festivities. The social prestige of this newly developing profession grew constantly.

Some of these dancing masters were highly learned men, and their treatises leave no doubt about their scholarly ambitions. Many of them were Jewish, descended from the Klesmorim, a group of medieval Jewish entertainers. The first dancing master known by name was Domenico da Piacenza, who in 1416 published the first European dance manual, *De arte saltandi et choreas ducendi* ("On the Art of Dancing and Directing Choruses"). His disciple, Antonio Cornazano, a nobleman by birth, became an immensely respected minister, educator of princes, court poet, and dancing master to the

Sforza family of Milan, where about 1460 he published his *Libro dell'arte del danzare* ("Book of the Art of the Dance"). Such books record little about the actual steps and the melodies to which they were performed, but they are eloquent in the description of the *balli*—works that were invented by the dancing masters themselves. Adapting steps from the various social dances, they used them in a kind of dance pantomime.

In France, numerous forms developed from the *branle*, a round dance of peasant origin that became fashionable in the courts. One of the most frequently mentioned of all the dances of the 15th century was the *morisca*, or moresque, a romanticized version of dances from Moorish Spain. These were first mentioned in 1446 by a Bohemian traveller who visited Burgos, Spain. Later, in Portugal, he encountered similar forms. Sometimes religious motifs of the legendary fight between Charlemagne and the Turkic invader Timur entered the *morisca*, but usually it was performed as a double-file choral dance. It had nothing to do, as was long believed, with the English masked Morris dance, now considered to be a survival from a primitive religious cult.

From such choral dances the ballet emerged. At the court entertainments throughout Savoy and northern Italy, sumptuous spectacles with mythological, symbolical, or allegorical content became increasingly popular. At these early stages, however, pantomime and dance are not easily distinguished. Famous examples of these spectacles are the presentation of the story of Jason and the Golden Fleece at the marriage of Philip the Good of Burgundy in 1430, and the dinner ballet on the same, though widely enlarged, subject staged for the wedding of the Duke of Milan in 1489.

Tudor England of the early 16th century had similar pageants, with the participants disguising "after the manner of Italie." Like the Italian *balli*, the English masque offered an almost unlimited choice of performing variations, from a simple dance in masks to the most elaborate spectacle interspersed with songs, speeches, and pantomimes. As for the actual dances, Robert Copland's *Maner of Dauncynge of Bace Daunces after the Use of Fraunce*, published in 1521 as an appendix to a French grammar, leaves no doubt that the English upper class of that period was thoroughly familiar with continental dance. But whereas the nobility preferred dances of slow, measured, and dignified stature, stylishly performed and modelled upon the standards of the French court, the peasants continued their boisterous dancing, in England as elsewhere, very much as they had for centuries.

In England in the late 16th century, Queen Elizabeth I gave dancing a further boost. She was a skilled practitioner of the galliard and the volta, with its tight embraces by high-leaping couples. She enjoyed watching the English country dances—the chain, ring,

The Elizabethan clown William Kempe (or Kemp) was renowned for dancing jigs. He gained notoriety for performing a Morris dance from London to Norwich, nearly 100 miles (161 kilometres) northward, in 1599. He is shown here with bells on his legs, dancing the Morris, while a man plays a pipe and drum.

and round dances of ancient origin and constantly new invention. These dances apparently provided a continuous infusion of new vitality into court dances. The nobles vied with one another in the execution of the jig, a sprightly and swift dance of "the folk" accompanied by songs. Dancing schools flourished everywhere in London, giving public displays and contributing considerably to the reputation of "the dancing English." Another extremely important contribution to dance was provided by Spain, which in the late 16th and early 17th centuries enjoyed a cultural renaissance. It was the "golden age" of Cervantes in literature, of Lope de Vega and Pedro Calderón de la Barca in the theatre, of El Greco and Diego Velázquez in painting. With the growth of Spain's empire in the Americas, dances of African American origin found their way back to Europe. The sarabande and the chaconne were brought from Central America before 1600. Both were considered outspokenly obscene in their suggestions of sexual encounters. They became extremely popular in the harbours of Andalusia, where they were polished and their pantomimic literalness somewhat moderated. From there they crossed the Pyrenees and were integrated into the canon of the French court dance.

Other dances from abroad played major roles in the shaping of Spain's national dances. The *canarie* of African origin certainly sired the Aragonese *jota*, while the sarabande brought forth the seguidilla. The Afro-Cuban *chica* lived on in the fandango, and the flamenco dances of the Andalusian Gypsies retained their Moorish heritage into the 20th century. It can be presumed that this influence on dances was not one way, that the European conquerors and colonists similarly influenced the dancing habits of the people in other lands.

# THE COUNTRY DANCE

The country dance is a genre of social dance for several couples, the characteristic form of folk and courtly dances of the British Isles. In England after about 1550, the term "country dancing" referred to a dance of the upper classes; similar dances, usually called traditional, existed contemporaneously among country people and persisted in popular tradition.

Country dances are performed in three characteristic formations: (1) circular, for an indefinite number of couples ("round" dances), (2) "longways" set, double-file line for an indefinite number of couples, men on one side, women on the other, and (3) geometric formations (*e.g.*, squares, triangles) or sets, usually for two, three, or four couples. The dancers execute a succession of varied patterns of figures. In "progressive-longways" dances, continuous interchange brings a new leading couple to the head of the set with each repetition of the pattern of figures. Round and longways dances predominate in the folk tradition. Longways and geometric sets are more frequent among courtly dances.

The patterns of the English country dances are similar to those of Irish set dances and of Scottish country dances such as reels and strathspeys. The step work of English dances, however, is simpler and the styling less formal.

Country dances from England were assimilated into the traditional dance of other countries—*e.g.,* Portugal and Denmark. English colonists carried them to North America, where they began a new folk-dance tradition as the "contra," or longways dance (*e.g.,* the Virginia reel), and, in modified form, as the American square dance.

Courtly dances also were exported from England. Longways and geometric sets appeared in Italy by the 15th century. The 18th-century French *contredanse* was at first based on English country dances and later evolved into independent varieties; by the 19th century it had spread to Germany and back to England. Although country dance originated as folk dance, the historical sources for its figures and music are urban and courtly: Italian (15th–16th century), English (16th–19th century), and French (18th century). The chief English source is John Playford's *The English Dancing Master* of 1650, continued in additional volumes until 1728 and critically revised in 1957 by M. J. Dean-Smith.

Cecil Sharp (1859–1924), founder of the English Folk Dance Society, made extensive

*(continued on the next page)*

*(continued from the previous page)*

**collections of rural country dances at a time when they were in danger of dying out and was largely responsible for their 20th-century revival. The Royal Scottish Country Dance Society has published traditional dances dating back to the 17th century and modern dances in traditional style. Popular country dances include the nonesuch, Hunsdon house, Morpeth rant, corn rigs, and old mole.**

## THE BIRTH OF BALLET

Out of the many styles in the late Middle Ages—religious dancing, folk dancing, and performances by minstrels—emerged the art form now known as ballet. An early pioneer whose work led in this direction was Guglielmo Ebreo, better known as William the Jew, from the Italian town of Pesaro. A teacher of dance to the nobility, he also wrote a study of dance that includes one of the first examples of recorded choreography. These dance steps were not designed for the stage or for professional dancers but for amateurs to perform at festive balls.

At the same time when William was active, dancing was on the move. First performed as part of feasts and then in ballrooms, dances finally found a home in theatres. Performed

The Valois Tapestries depict a 1573 ball or festival in honour of the Polish ambassadors at the court of Catherine de Médicis (Medici, in Italian), who is wearing black and seated at the center. Members of the court can be seen dancing before the queen. For the spectacle, Balthazar de Beaujoyeulx, Catherine's Italian dance master, created a *ballet de cour*, the Ballet des Polonais, and presented it in the Tuileries Palace in Paris.

between the acts of classical comedies, tragedies, or operas, they became known as intermezzos. Gradually the word *balletti*, which originally referred to dances performed in ball-rooms, was used for the dramatic works in theatres. Ballet as it is known now was just around the corner.

Meanwhile, dance became the subject of serious studies in France. A group of writers call-ing themselves La Pléiade aimed for a revival of the theatre of the ancient Greeks with its music, song, and dance. In Catherine de Médicis (1519–89), the Florentine wife of Henry II, king of France, the Italian dancing masters found an influential sponsor in Paris. She called to Paris the Italian musician and dancing master Balt-azarini di Belgioioso, who changed his name to Balthazar de Beaujoyeulx (early 16th century to 1587). There had been previous fetes in both France and Italy that offered masquerades, pantomimes, and dances with allegorical and symbolic subjects, but none of them compared to the splendours of the *Ballet comique de la reine* that Beaujoyeulx staged in 1581 for Cath-erine.

This "ballet" told the story of the legendary sorceress Circe and her evil deeds. Spoken texts alternated with dances amid magnificently decorative settings. The performers, recruited from the nobility, moved on the floor more like animated costumes than individual danc-ers. They came together in strikingly designed groups, and they set up geometrical floor patterns that had highly symbolic meanings. (To audiences of the period, for example, three concentric circles represented Perfect Truth, and two equilateral triangles within a circle stood for Supreme Power.) The ballet, which ended in an act of homage to the royal majesties present, had a distinct political moral. Circe had to render her might to the absolutist power of the king of France as the supreme symbol of a peaceful and harmonious world.

The *Ballet comique* launched the species known as *ballet de cour,* in which the monarchs themselves participated. The idealized dances represented the supreme order that France itself, suffering from internal wars, lacked so badly. The steps were those of the social dances of the times, but scholars became aware of how these native materials might be used to propagate the Greek revival. They thoroughly analyzed and systematized the dances, and in 1588 the priest Jehan Tabourot, writing under the pen name Thoinot Arbeau, published his *Orchésographie,* which he subtitled "a treatise in dialogue form by which everyone can easily learn and practice the honest exercise of the dance." This was the first book containing reliable descriptions of how, and to what kind of music, the *basse danse,* pavane, galliard, *volta,* courante, allemande, gavotte, *canarie, bouffon,* moresque, and 23 different variations of the *branle* were performed.

# CHAPTER TWO

# THE 17TH, 18TH, AND 19TH CENTURIES

Under kings Louis XIV and Louis XV, France led western Europe into the age of the rococo in the arts. The rococo began as a movement toward simplicity and naturalness, a reaction against the stilted mannerisms and preciousness to which the earlier baroque art was considered to have degenerated. It was a great age of and for dancing, with the minuet the symbol of its emphasis on civilized movement. This formal dance, the perfect execution of which was almost a science in itself, reflected the rococo idea of naturalness. The statement that "the dance has now come to the highest point of its perfection" by the composer Jean-Philippe Rameau (1683–1764) suggested how conscious the French were of the great strides dance had made. That this was particularly the case in France was confirmed by the English poet and essayist Soame Jenyns (1704–87) in his lines "None will sure presume to rival France, / Whether she forms or executes the dance." None, however, excelled the estimation of his profession by the dancing master in Molière's *Le Bourgeois Gentilhomme* (1670):

> There is nothing so necessary to human beings as the dance . . . Without the dance, a man would not be able to do anything. . . . All the misfortunes of man, all the baleful reverses with which histories are filled, the blunders of politicians and the failures of great leaders, all of this is the result of not knowing how to dance.

# THE MATURING OF BALLET

Dance was finally deemed ready for an academy of its own. In 1661, 13 dancing masters who had been members of a professional guild of medieval origin, together with some musicians, composers, and the makers of instruments, were granted a charter by Louis XIV for the Académie Royale de Danse.

## TECHNICAL CODIFICATIONS AND DANCE SCHOLARSHIP

The academicians were charged with setting up objective standards for perfecting of their arts, with unifying the rules of dance training, and with issuing licenses to dancing instructors. Though the nobility continued for some time to participate in the *ballets de cour*, and Louis himself danced in them until 1669, the dance became more and more the province of highly trained specialists.

After 1700 ballet and social dance took separate paths. But while the ballet continued to absorb new ideas from the folk and social dance, its practitioners and theoreticians looked down on those more common forms. A profusion of books on dance began to appear—treatises, instructions, and analyses as well as the first attempts to record dances by means of written notation. The first history of dance was Claude-François Menestrier's *Des ballets anciens et modernes* (“On Dances Ancient and Modern”; 1682).

The second major work of European dance literature, after Arbeau's *Orchésographie*, was Raoul Feuillet's *Chorégraphie, ou l'art de décrire la danse* (“Choreography, or the Art of Describing the Dance”; 1700). It became the standard grammar for the dances practiced at the turn of the century, describing them in minute detail and notating them by a system devised by Feuillet. This indicated the position of the feet and directions, combinations, and floor patterns of the steps and leaps. The notations system was unable, however, to register the movements of the upper parts of

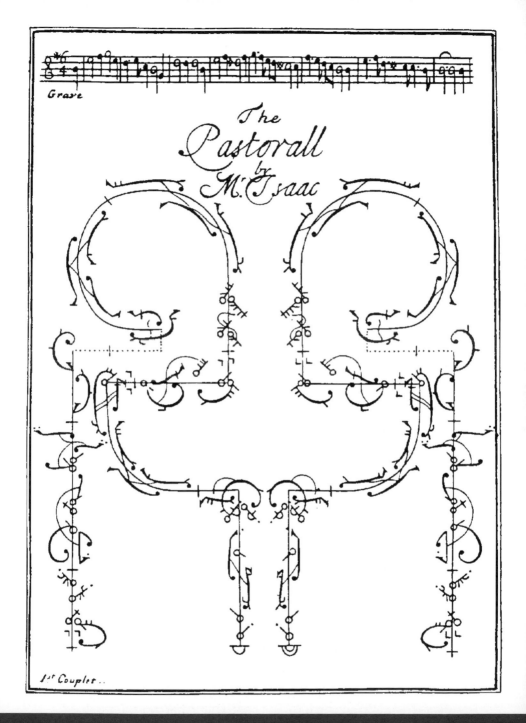

A page from Raoul Feuillet's *Chorégraphie, ou l'art de décrire la danse* ("Choreography, or the Art of Describing the Dance"; 1700) illustrates the dance notation system originated by Feuillet's teacher Pierre Beauchamp. Dance steps traced on the floor formed the basis of the system.

the body. Feuillet provided as well a complete definition of the principles of the dance first described by the Académie in the 1660s. These included the *en dehors* (*i.e.*, the turnout of the body and its limbs), the five classical positions of the feet (heels touching and feet forming a straight line; heels apart and feet forming a straight line; one foot in front of the other with the heel against the instep; feet apart, one in front of the other; and one foot in front of the other with the heel against the joint of the big toe), the port de bras (*i.e.*, the positions and movements of the arms and hands), and the leaps to the *grande élévation*, the aerial movements of the dance.

In 1706 Feuillet's influential book was translated into English by John Weaver (1673–1760), a dancer, choreographer, and teacher who worked mainly at the Drury Lane Theatre, London. In 1717 he produced one of the first serious ballets without words, *The Loves of Mars and Venus.* Weaver was the first dance teacher to insist that dance instructors have a thorough knowledge of human anatomy. In 1721 he published his *Anatomical and Mechanical Lectures upon Dancing*, which became a standard work of international importance. Germany also was represented in the field of dance scholarship, most notably by Leipzig Gottfried Tauber in *Der rechtschaffene Tanzlehrer* ("The Correctly Working Dance Teacher"; 1717). These books strongly emphasized the contributions of dance to general education and manners. In this period dance was considered the basis of all education, and well-to-do parents went to great pains to have their children properly instructed.

## VARIETIES OF THE BALLET

As the technical demands of performance became greater and the amateurs gave way to the professionals, performance of the ballet moved from the dance floor onto the stage. There it gradually shed its declamations and its songs and concentrated on telling a story through the gestures of dance and mime alone. But this purifying process took time. For decades different forms of mixed-media spectacles were seen, from the *comédies-ballets* of Molière (1622–73) and the composer Jean-Baptiste Lully (1632–87) to the *opéras-ballets* of André Campra (1660–1744) and Rameau, which were successions of songs and dances on a common theme. The first ballet to be performed without the diversions of speech or song was *Le Triomphe de l'amour* (*The Triumph of Love*; 1681), choreographed by Charles-Louis Beauchamp (1636–c. 1719) to Lully's music. Originally a *ballet de cour,* it was revived for the stage with a professional cast. Its star, Mademoiselle Lafontaine, became ballet's first *première danseuse* exactly 100 years after the *Ballet comique* had been produced.

An even more dramatic form known as *ballet d'action* came into being in 1708, when two professional dancers presented an entire scene from the tragedy *Horace* by Pierre Corneille (1606–84) in dance and mime. Weaver's silent ballets, whose expressive dance much impressed English audiences, also encouraged Marie Sallé, a highly ambitious dramatic dancer. Despairing of the *opéras-ballets* of Paris, she went to London, where she performed in pantomimes and produced a miniature dance-drama of her own, *Pygmalion* (1734). In it she appeared in a flimsy muslin dress and loose, flowing hair rather than the heavy costumes and elaborate wigs usually worn by ballerinas. Thus lightened, the dancer was able to move with much greater freedom.

## EARLY VIRTUOSOS OF THE DANCE

The era of the great dancer was at hand. Marie Sallé (1707–56) was the greatest dancer-mime and an important innovator of her day. Her popularity was rivalled by the Brussels-born Marie Camargo (1710–70), who excelled Sallé in lightness and sparkle. She used the entrechat, a series of rapid crossings of the legs that previously had been used only by male dancers. To show off properly her entrechats and other lithe footwork, she shortened her skirt by several inches, thereby contributing to costume reform. Both ballerinas were depicted by

Nicolas Lancret (1690–1743), a painter known for his festive scenes, and both were praised by the writer and philosopher Voltaire (1694–1778), who carefully compared their respective virtues. Both, however, were surpassed by the Italian dancer Barberina Campanini (1721–99), whose fame is less adequately recorded in dance history. By 1739, she had taken Paris by storm, demonstrating jumps and turns executed with a speed and brilliance hitherto unknown. She offered ample proof that the Italian school of dance teaching had by no means died out with the earlier exodus of so many of its best practitioners to the French courts. Despite the great public acclaim that these ballerinas attracted, they were overshadowed by Louis Dupré (1697–1744), known as the Great Dupré and the god of the dance. In grace, majesty, and allure, he was unsurpassed, giving the male dancer a prominence he held for a century. Dupré was also the first of a direct line of great dance teachers that was unbroken in the late 20th century. Gaétan Vestris (1729–1808), who studied under Dupré at the Paris Opéra ballet school, was appointed a soloist in 1751 and enjoyed a succession of triumphs in ballets of Jean-Barthélemy Lany, Pierre Gardel, and Jean-Georges Noverre. Because of his conceited ways, as well as his undisputed gifts, he was called, half ironically, the god of the dance.

# MARIE CAMARGO, BALLERINA

Marie-Anne de Cupis de Camargo, known as Marie Camargo, was born on April 15, 1710, in Brussels, Spanish Netherlands (now in Belgium). Camargo studied in Paris under Françoise Prévost and danced in Brussels and Rouen before her Paris Opéra debut in 1726 in *Les Caractères de la danse.* Her success provoked the jealousy of her aging teacher, Prévost, who relegated her to the ensemble. She soon won an unexpected triumph, however, by improvising a spectacular solo when another dancer failed to enter on cue. Camargo went on to consolidate her success, setting fashion trends in shoes and coiffures and eventually dancing in 78 ballets and operas. Among her many admirers was the Count de Clermont, with whom she lived when she temporarily retired from the stage (1735–41). Camargo's final retirement was in 1751. Camargo died on April 20, 1770, in Paris.

She reputedly established the ballet's basic leg position as turned-out 90° from the hip. A rival of Marie Sallé, Camargo was noted for her speed and agility and for her perfection of the entrechat and cabriole, jumping steps previously executed chiefly

Nicolas Lancret painted *Mademoiselle de Camargo Dancing* in 1730. One of Camargo's innovations was shortening her costume so that her unusually difficult footwork could be seen by the audience.

by men. To obtain the necessary freedom of movement and to display her rapidly moving feet, she became the first danseuse to shorten her ballet skirts to calf length, to remove the heels from ballet slippers, and to wear close-fitting drawers (that evolved into ballet's basic "tights") while dancing.

# THE REIGN OF THE MINUET

In the realm of the social dance, the years between 1650 and 1750 were called the age of the minuet by the dance and music historian Curt Sachs.

## THE FRENCH DANCE SUITE

At the great balls of the French court at Versailles, the minuet was the high point of the festivities, which culminated in a suite of dances. The opening *branle*, led by the king and his escort, was a measured circling around, one couple after another. Next came the courante, which had been toned down from its earlier rather capricious figurations. Over the years it assumed a continuously greater dignity until it was danced with such gravity and sobriety that it was termed the doctor dance. It went quickly out of fashion, however, after 1700. Following the courante in the succession was the gavotte, which opened in the form of a round dance. A couple separated to each perform a short solo, then returned to the original circle. Sometimes the suite was extended through an allemande (French: "German"), an old dance form that was introduced into France from the heavily German-speaking province of Alsace in the 1680s. This dance, with its turning couples, the lady on the arm of the gentleman, was a relative of the German *Ländler* and a precursor of the waltz.

## FORM OF THE MINUET

But the unrivalled king of the social dances was the minuet, named from the *pas menu* ("small step"), a term used at least as early as the 15th century. The earliest surviving specimen was composed by Lully in 1663. Mozart composed a series of 12 minuets as late as 1789. The minuet originated as a folk dance in Poitou, but as a court dance it took its form from the courante. Though today it looks mannered, even artificial, in its time it was looked upon as the most beautiful and harmonious of dances, and to execute it perfectly required prolonged and careful study:

> The minuet was performed in open couples; spectators and partners were saluted with ceremonial bows. With dainty little steps and glides, to the right and to the left, forward and backward, in quarter turns, approaching and retreating hand in hand, searching and evading, now side by side, now facing, now gliding past one another, the ancient dance play of courtship appears here in a last and almost unrecognizable stylization and refinement.
>
> (Curt Sachs, *World History of the Dance,* trans. Bessie Schönberg, W.W. Norton & Co., Inc., 1937.)

In spite of the great popularity of the minuet before the French Revolution, it was the object of much barbed commentary in the late 18th century. Voltaire compared the metaphysical philosophers of his time with the dancers of the minuet, who, in their elegant attire, bow and mince daintily across the room showing off their charms, move without progressing a single step, and end up at the very spot from which they began.

## ENGLISH SOCIAL DANCE

England thoroughly democratized

A group of revelers dance the minuet in Giovanni Battista Tiepolo's painting *The Minuet* (1756).

the dance. Though the English Puritanism of the 17th century stigmatized dance as one of man's most sinful occupations, even Oliver Cromwell, lord protector of England under the Puritan rule in the 1650s, could not prevent the appearance of *The English Dancing Master* (issued 1650; dated 1651), by the bookseller and publisher John Playford (1623–c. 1686). This was a collection of English traditional dances and tunes. It had 18 editions in 80 years, each one adding to the repertoire. Its 900 choral dances of rustic origin, which formerly had been danced in the open air but were now usually performed indoors, included an enormous variety of forms and patterns. It was written in straightforward, matter-of-fact language, with no discrimination of dances by social class. Its instructions could be understood and its dances performed by anyone. People could enjoy dancing as a playful, sportive activity rather than as an exercise of courtly etiquette.

These "country dances" could as well be city dances, as is suggested by such names as "Mayden Lane" and "Hide Park" from London locales. Others were named for persons—"Parson's farewell" and "My Lady Foster's delight"—and that there were foreign influences can be surmised from the names the "Spanish Jeepsie" and "a la mode de France." At the same time, native jigs and hornpipes continued to flourish. The English were particularly fond of the Morris dance. This dance may have received its name from the blackened faces of some of its participants, suggestive of the African Moors, but its origins were in the ancient ritual dances. It was a vigorous male dance, in the form of a dance procession through town streets. Its participants, in the disguises of such popular characters as the fool or the Queen of May, wore jingling bells around their ankles and sometimes galloped about on hobby-horses. Other dancers wore antlers, tails, and similar animal masking.

About 1700 the English country dances began to appear on the Continent, where they were somewhat formalized and sometimes substantially altered. In France they were named *contredanses*. The longways, dances with double lines of dancers facing one another, became *contredanses anglaises*; the rounds became the *contredanses françaises*, which were also known as cotillions and quadrilles. These figure dances, which quickly spread to Spain, Germany, Poland, and other countries, were the dances of the rising middle class. By no means revolutionary in their content, they were nonetheless a distinct declaration of rationality and common sense in dance, a counterbalance to the artificialities and mannerisms of the aristocratic court dances. The orthodox dance teachers might bemoan the decline from the standards that were epitomized in the minuet, but the townspeople and peasants, unconcerned with such niceties, continued in their uncomplicated knowledge that dancing could be fun.

# DANCE IN EARLY AMERICA

As known today, social dancing is an activity that can be traced back to three sources: the courts of Europe, international society, and primitive cultures. Among noblemen and women of 16th- and 17th-century Europe, ballroom dancing was a popular diversion. After the political upheavals of the 18th and 19th centuries, dances once performed by the aristocracy alone became popular among ordinary people as well. In America, too, dances that were once confined to the gentry who first led the republic passed to the common folk. By the mid-19th century, popular dances attracted many participants who performed minuets, quadrilles, polkas, and waltzes—all of European origin.

## ATTITUDES IN COLONIAL AMERICA

The English colonists in America had mixed opinions about dance. There was the complete disapproval of those who saw only its inherent licentiousness, but from others came at least a tacit toleration of the obviously irrepressible urge to dance. The South, more heavily populated by colonists with aristocratic backgrounds, was generally more inclined to dance than the North, where religious fervour had motivated much of the migration from England. But what was allowed and even encouraged in Connecticut was strictly forbidden in Massachusetts. The general consensus was apparently that dancing in itself was not bad, but that no punishment could be severe enough for what was regarded as lascivious dancing. The Quakers, who had settled mainly in Pennsylvania, were very much against dancing, and in 1706 they complained bitterly about a dancing and fencing school being tolerated in Philadelphia. They feared that the school's teachings would tend to corrupt their children.

## EXTERNAL AND INTERNAL INFLUENCES

Nonetheless, Playford's *The English Dancing Master* was by no means unknown in America. There were also dancing masters and dancing mistresses to instruct in and lead the dances that had been brought from the Old World. There were society balls in the cities along the coast, and on the inland frontiers the settlers of the widely scattered farmsteads often came together for exuberant feasting and social dancing. Here dancing was considered a socializing virtue expressed in this anonymous observation:

I really know among us of no custom which is so useful and tends so much to establish the union and the little society which subsists among us. Poor as we are, if we have not the gorgeous balls, the harmonious concerts, the shrill horn of Europe, yet we delight our hearts as well with the simple negro fiddle.

What the colonists saw of American Indian dancing they found very strange and primitive, and there was virtually no exchange of dancing customs between the groups. The situation differed, however, with regard to the black slaves, who in the 17th century had brought their own songs and dances from their native lands in Africa.

During religious holidays in New Amsterdam, blacks danced in the streets to the musical accompaniment of three-stringed fiddles and drums constructed from eel pots and covered with sheepskins. Dutch families joined in the festivities. When New Amsterdam became New York, however, the English discouraged dancing between whites and blacks; blacks went on to develop the characteristic dance style that would so deeply affect social dancing in the 19th and 20th centuries.

Early in the 18th century, rather rough theatrical entertainments, acts of acrobatic skill or pantomimes in which dances played an increasing role, began to spread through

James Oglethorpe, a founder of the British colony of Georgia, watches the local American Indians dance during a meeting in Savannah in the mid-1730s.

the American colonies. These often amateurish showings got a mighty boost when the first professional companies came from Europe, about the middle of the century, to perform plays and harlequinades with incidental dances.

# THE RISE OF THE WALTZ

The age of the minuet was followed by that of the waltz. As the French Revolution approached, the minuet, a form that exuded the essence of earlier decades, died a natural death. The English country dances, expressing the self-satisfaction of the bourgeoisie, fared little better.

## THE ROMANTIC MOVEMENT IN DANCE

The young people, whose preferences led the way in creating new forms, had lived through the revolutionary events of the 1780s and '90s. They now looked to dance as a way to unleash deeper emotion, to satisfy the needs of body and soul, and to mobilize more vital and dynamic expression than that permitted by the sober and decorous rules of the dancing masters. The overflow of feeling and the striving for horizons broader than those understood by the traditional canons of French rationalism were among the factors that generated the Romantic movement in the arts of Europe. This new direction was clearly expressed in the waltz, a dance filled with the Dionysian spirit.

Like much of the spirit of the Romantic movement, the waltz was of German origin. It paralleled the Sturm und Drang movement in German literature, which featured the new forms of prose and poetry by Johann von Goethe and Friedrich Schiller. One of the most glowing advocates of the waltz was Goethe, who time and again praised it, nowhere more than in his novel *Die Leiden des Jungen Werthers* (1774; *The Sorrows of Werter,* 1779): "Never have I moved so lightly. I was no longer a human being. To hold the most adorable creature in one's arms and fly around with her like the wind, so that everything around us fades away." Even the aristocrats who formed the Congress of Vienna in 1815, which sought to restore law and order to Europe following the upheavals brought on by Napoleon, delighted in performing this earliest of all nonaristocratic ballroom dances.

## SPREAD OF THE WALTZ

The waltz started as a turning dance of couples. It was especially popular in south Germany and Austria, where it was known under such different names as *Dreher, Ländler,* and *Deutscher.* More than any other dance it appeared to represent some of the abstract values of the new era, the ideals of freedom, character, passion, and expressiveness. This may explain somewhat its eruption into the limelight of international popularity. This popularity was scaled in 1787 when it was brought to operatic stage. Vienna became the city of the waltz, for there it surpassed everything in wild fury. It swept over national frontiers, and in 1804 the French were reported to be passionately in love with this light, gliding dance. "A waltz, another waltz" was the common cry from the ballroom floor, for the French could not get enough of the dance.

Some guardians of the public morality disapproved of the "mad whirling" of the waltz and it did not arrive in England until 1812. At the Prussian court in Berlin it was forbidden until 1818, though Queen Luise had danced it while still a princess in 1794. The guardians could do no more than delay its total victory, and it conquered the world without sanction of courts, of dancing masters, or of other powers. After many centuries of leadership, France no longer set the fashions. In 1819 Carl Maria von Weber's *Invitation to the Dance* represented the declaration of love of classical music to the waltz. Shortly thereafter began the age of the Viennese waltz kings, most notably expressed by the Strauss family.

Couples are depicted dancing the rapid, whirling Viennese waltz in this drawing from the 19th century. The word *waltz* is from German *walzen*, which means "to revolve."

## OFFSPRING AND RIVALS

The waltz sired a great variety of offspring throughout Europe. Germany developed such variations of the waltz as the schottische, with turns like those of the waltz. France had its airy *balance valse*, and the Americans later on had their Boston waltz, a slower, gliding variant. About 1840 a serious rival to the waltz emerged in the polka, a Bohemian dance that took its name from the Czech word *půlka*, "half step." It was full of fiery vigour. Another Bohemian folk dance finding favour in the dance halls was the *rejdovák* or *redowa*, while Poland's mazurka and *krakowiak* enjoyed great popularity. No ball could be concluded without a galop, in which couples galloped through the hall with accelerated polka steps, an exhausting exercise that required consider-able reserves of stamina.

# FOUNDATIONS OF MODERN BALLET

The ideals of naturalness, character, soul, passion, and expressiveness came to govern the ballet.

## NOVERRE AND HIS CONTEMPORARIES

The French dancer-choreographer-teacher Jean-Georges Noverre (1727–1810) was the first major reformer of ballet. He defined his artistic positions in *Lettres sur la danse et sur les ballets* (*Letters on Dancing and Ballets*), published in 1760 and continuously reprinted ever since. He worked in Paris, London, Stutt-gart, and Vienna, and his influence spread as far as St. Petersburg. He preached the dignity of the ballet and tried to purge it of its excessive artificialities and conventions. He choreographed subjects of mythology and history in highly dramatic narrative forms. He collaborated with some of the major composers of the period, including Mozart, on his ballets.

Jean-Baptiste Perronneau drew this pastel on paper of Jean-Georges Noverre in 1764. Noverre, a distinguished French choreographer, stressed the importance of dramatic motivation, which he called *ballet d'action*, and decried the overemphasis on technical virtuosity.

Noverre was not alone, and the others around him were full of the same zest to give a new meaning to ballet. In Vienna he had a feud with the Italian choreographer Gasparo Angiolini (1731–1803) over Noverre's reforms of the *ballet d'action*. Angiolini claimed these for his teacher, the Austrian choreographer Franz Hilverding (1710–68). In Bordeaux, Noverre's pupil Jean Dauberval premiered in 1789 *La Fille mal gardée* (*The*

*Ill-Guarded Maiden*), usually called *Vain Precautions* in English, which became the first durable ballet comedy. It introduced the *demi-caractère* dance, which featured what were considered to be "true-to-life" characters. In London, still another pupil, Charles Didelot, created in 1796 *Flore et Zéphyre*. This was the first attempt to bestow on the individual dances within the ballet a certain period and local coloration and to break the uniformity of step and movement of the corps de ballet by assigning individual tasks to its various members. Later, Didelot thoroughly reformed the ballet school in St. Petersburg, which had existed since 1738. There he also created the first ballets of the Russian national repertory. Among these were the first ballets to be based on the works of the Russian writer Aleksandr Pushkin (1799–1837), whose stories continued to be used as ballet libretti for many decades.

In Milan, Salvatore Viganò, who had worked under Dauberval and Didelot and who had choreographed in 1801 the first performance of Beethoven's *Creatures of Prometheus*, was praised by the French writer Stendhal for his thrilling ballets based, among other subjects, on Shakespeare's *Othello* and *Coriolanus*. He was followed by Carlo Blasis, who was more noted as a teacher and theoretician. His *Traité élémentaire, théorique, et pra-*

*tique de l'art de la danse* (1820; *Elementary Treatise upon the Theory and Practice of the Art of Dancing*) became the standard work of ballet teaching for the 19th century. In 1837 he founded the Imperial Ballet Academy, through which Milan became, with Paris and St. Petersburg, a third ballet centre of world renown.

## THE ROMANTIC BALLET

During the 1830s and '40s the Romantic movement flooded ballet stages with nature spirits, fairies, and sylphids. The cult of the ballerina replaced that of the male dancer, whose last and greatest representative had been the Italian-born French dancer Gaétan Vestris (1729–1808). The techniques of female dancing were greatly improved. Skirts were shortened further, and blocked shoes permitted toe dancing. Choreographers strove for a more expressive vocabulary and highlighted the individual qualities of their dancers.

*La Sylphide* (1836) stated a main subject of the Romantic ballet, the fight between the real world and the spiritual world. This theme was enhanced and expanded in *Giselle* (1841) and *Ondine* (1843). Paris and London were the taste setters, and it was London that in 1845 witnessed the *Pas de quatre*, for which the French choreographer Jules Perrot brought together, for four performances, four of the greatest ballerinas of the day, the Italians Marie Taglioni (1804–84), Carlotta Grisi (1819–99), and Fanny Cerrito (1817–1909), and Lucile Grahn (1819–1907). After this the decline of Romantic ballet was rapid, at least in these cities. It continued to flourish into the early 1860s, however, in Copenhagen under the choreographer Auguste Bournonville, whose repertoire was kept alive by the Royal Danish Ballet into the second half of the 20th century. Russia, under the French-born Marius Petipa (1819–1910) and his Russian aide Lev Ivanov (1834–1901), built a world-famous ballet culture of its own. Linked at first with Paris, it gradually developed its own balletic idiom from native as well as imported sources. The high point of the classical ballet under the tsars was reached with the St. Petersburg productions of *The Sleeping Beauty* (1890), *The Nutcracker* (1892), and *Swan Lake* (1895), all with music composed by Pyotr Ilyich Tchaikovsky, and *Raymonda* (1898), composed by Aleksandr Glazunov (1865–1936). While the ballet prospered in St. Petersburg and Moscow, it waned in Paris. Its ballerinas even appeared in male roles, as in *Coppélia* (1870). In Milan the extravaganzas of Luigi Manzotti (1838–1905) offered anything but dancing while glorifying the progress of mankind through material discov-

A Russian photographer took this photograph of a scene from the first performance of Pyotr Ilyich Tchaikovsky's ballet *The Sleeping Beauty* at the Mariinsky Theatre in St. Petersburg in 1890.

eries and inventions.

The 19th century also saw an unprecedented increase in travel and in cross-cultural influences. Many seemingly exotic dance styles arrived on the Western scene. Troupes from as far as India and Japan appeared at expositions in Paris and London, starting a lively interest in folk and ethnic dancing. Ballerinas of the Romantic ballet travelled from one European city to another, from Milan to London to Moscow. The Austrian dancer Fanny Elssler toured the Americas in the early 1840s for two years, visiting Havana twice. The great choreographers, too, went from city to city. The language of dance became a medium of international communication without regard for difference in geography or spoken language.

# THEATRE AND BALLROOM DANCE

Other dance entertainments of a lighter kind gained immense popularity during the 19th century. In Paris the all-female cancan became the rage. Its electrifying high kicks were shockingly exhibitionistic and titillating. After 1844 it became a feature of the music halls, of revues, and of operetta. It was raised to musical prominence by operetta composer Jacques Offenbach (1819–80) and vividly depicted by the painter Henri de Toulouse-Lautrec (1864–1901). London enjoyed the Alhambra and Empire ballets, which were mostly classical ballets with spectacular productions. But it was America that provided the widest variety. There were patriotic spectacles, popular after the Revolutionary War, such as *The Patriot, or Liberty Asserted*, in which dance figured prominently.

More important and of longer range results were the minstrel shows, extravaganzas, burlesques, and vaudevilles. These represented a confluence of a wide assortment of dance and theatrical influences, especially from black culture. White men affected black faces and black dances, and black men affected the faces and dances of whites. Dances were tap and soft-shoe, the buck-and-wing, and similar routines. Theatrical productions offered all kinds of dance, from European-imported ballets through entirely native exhibitions of female beauty verging on the striptease. American dancers began to establish reputations both in America and Europe. The ballerina Augusta Maywood (1825–76?) was the first American dancer to perform at the Paris Opéra.

During the 19th century there was also an enormous increase in the number of public ballrooms and other dancing establishments in the fast-growing cities of the West. Here were first encountered American imports such as the barn dance, then called the military schottische; the Washington post, a very rapid two-step in march formation; and the cakewalk, which contorted the body to degrees previously unknown. For the first time Europe found in the New World a new infusion of blood for its dancing veins. The tempo of the dances quickened, reflecting

# AUGUSTA MAYWOOD

Augusta Williams was born in 1825, probably in New York City. She was the first American ballerina to achieve international renown.

Augusta Williams was the daughter of itinerant English actors. She acquired the name of her stepfather, the theatrical manager Robert Campbell Maywood, when she was three. She began studying ballet under Paul H. Hazard in 1836, and in 1837 she made her public debut in *The Maid of Cashmere* (Marie Taglioni's ballet from Daniel Auber's opera *Le Dieu et la Bayadère*). She and her costar, fellow student Mary Ann Lee, were a great success. Enthusiastic audiences encouraged a rivalry between the two dancers, and in March 1838 the two appeared together in *The Dew Drop, or La Sylphide*, a version of Taglioni's *La Sylphide*, in New York City.

In May 1838 Maywood's stepfather took her to Paris, where she studied under Jean Coralli and Joseph Mazilier, respectively ballet master and principal dancer at the Paris Opéra. In November 1839 she made her Paris debut at the Opéra in Coralli's *Le Diable Boîteux* and was a great popular and critical success. In 1840 she eloped with the dancer Charles Mabille. They returned to Paris and were legally married, but, their Opéra contracts broken, they were consigned over the next five years to dancing engagements in venues around Marseille and Lyon, France; Lisbon, Portugal; and other smaller cities. In 1845 Maywood left Mabille and went to Vienna, where she danced with great success at the Kärntnertor Theatre until late in 1847. After a short engagement in Budapest, she went to Milan in 1848 and made her La Scala debut. At age 23 she became prima ballerina at La Scala, where she remained until her retirement in 1862.

Among the ballets in which Maywood appeared are *Giselle, La Gypsy, Faust,* and, after she began touring with her own company—she was the first ballerina to do so—her own ballet versions of Harriet Beecher Stowe's *Uncle Tom's Cabin* and Filippo Termanini's *Rita Gauthier,* the latter based on Alexandre Dumas *fils's La Dame aux camélias.* She married Carlo Gardini, an Italian physician, journalist, and impresario, in 1858 and retired from the stage four years later. They settled in Vienna, where

*(continued on the next page)*

*(continued from the previous page)*

**she opened a school of ballet. She taught until 1873 and in later years lived in northern Italy on Lake Como. Maywood died on November 3, 1876, in Lwów, Poland, Austrian Empire [now Lviv, Ukraine]).**

perhaps the quickening pace of life and the great social changes of the century.

## EARLY BALLROOM DANCE AND INVITATIONAL EVENTS

Ballroom dance, a type of social dancing, was originally practiced in Europe and the United States, and is performed by couples and follows prescribed steps. The tradition was historically distinguished from folk or country dance by its association with the elite social classes and with invitational dance events.

The social origin of ballroom dance lies in the European court dances of the 17th and 18th centuries, although many of the dance steps were adapted from folk traditions. Initially, court dances were performed facing the throne, a practice known as "fronting the state," because it was unacceptable to turn one's back on a ruler. As court etiquette relaxed in the 19th century, however, dancers were required to face the ruler only on the most formal occasions or when they were being presented to the court. Otherwise participants danced in circles or squares throughout the ballroom.

During the first half of the 19th century, most ballroom dances, such as the polka and the waltz, were an integral component of social events known as assemblies—planned evenings for a limited group of invitees connected through family, neighbourhood, or affiliation, such as a regiment or a hunting group. Socially respected figures, such as the patriarch of a landowning family, the master of the hunt, or the colonel of the local regiment, were the usual sponsors of these events, and strict rules of etiquette were followed throughout the evening. For dancing, each woman was given a decorative souvenir card on which to list her partner for each dance; following protocol, a man would wait to be introduced to a young woman before asking for permission to enter his name on her dance card. Descriptions of behaviour and expectations at such events are settings for key plot developments in many 19th-century novels, notably those by Jane Austen, Henry James, Louisa May Alcott, Gustave Flaubert, and Leo Tolstoy.

At a typical assembly, dances were performed to live music in a specific order that was set and announced by the orchestra leader. Faster dances, such as galops and polkas, alternated with slower ones. The music was frequently adapted from operas, ballets, or national folk (or folk-derived) dances, such as the Polish mazurka, polonaise, or *cracovienne*. Published music for social dance was frequently named for celebrities or special events. Although dance formations ultimately depended on the dimensions of the ballroom, most assemblies included circle (or round) dances as well as various dances generically known as germans, which were performed by lines of couples. Steps to the dances were usually learned from older family members or from friends, or occasionally from teachers, who were frequently also musicians. Dance manuals, which were published by music engravers, were also available. The steps of ballroom dances were much like those of other social dances, but the settings, social class associations, and social protocol of the two traditions differed radically. Indeed, events held in public dance halls and concert salons were commercial—rather than invitational—initiatives, and they did not adhere to the elaborate systems of etiquette that governed ballrooms.

The structure of ballroom dance events changed significantly during the later 19th century, particularly in terms of the structure of dance events and styles performed, as well as the transmission of the tradition. Invitational events were organized for a select few, such as New York City's so-called Astor 400—the popular label applied to the invitation list for social leader Caroline Schermerhorn Astor's Patriarch Ball (c. 1872–91). Such events combined a reception, at least one repast, and lengthy dance sets that alternated round dances with an elaborate type of german called the cotillion. The cotillion consisted of a series of short dances or dance segments that mimicked social behaviour, with couples presenting each other with flowers or souvenirs, for example. By the end of the 19th century the cotillion had become so commonplace that its name had come to designate the ballroom dance event itself.

Not only did the style of ballroom dance change in the 19th century, but so too did its mode of transmission. In the 1870s individuals as well as families established studios and joined professional associations to teach steps, patterns, and musicality, thus stabilizing the profession of dance master. The association that later became the Dance Masters of America was founded in 1884. Certain dance masters, such as Allen Dodworth and his family in New York and A. E. Bournique in Chicago, were favoured by the social elite.

Meanwhile, the printing and distribution of dance manuals moved from music engravers to publishers of self-help books, etiquette books, women's magazines, and clothing pattern books such as those issued by the company of Ebenezer Butterick. Books aimed at potential invitees were often miniaturized to fit in a pocket or a small handbag. A separate line of manuals and a growing number of professional periodicals were sold to dance masters and to cotillion leaders, who managed the order of dances and other activities during the evening.

# CHAPTER THREE

# THE 20TH AND 21ST CENTURIES

Ballroom dances and dance events were transformed monumentally—and indeed, democratized—with the social shifts of the early 20th century. Dances such as one-steps, two-steps, hesitations, and trots—all so named because of their generally faster and more strongly syncopated (with accents placed on normally weak beats) musical style—could be learned by the public at large from teachers, manuals, or general-interest newspaper and magazine columns.

## BALLROOM DANCE IN THE EARLY PART OF THE 20TH CENTURY

In this new atmosphere of accessibility, two subcategories developed: professional exhibition ballroom dancing, in which a couple was paid to demonstrate in front of a paying audience, and competitive ballroom dance, in which amateur couples performed within strict regulations for prizes or titles.

Exhibition ballroom dancers were marketed not only as performers but also as teachers and choreographers. Championed by Vernon and Irene Castle (with their manager Elisabeth Marbury), these professional duos were promoted through photographs, films, and their endorsement of sheet music and recordings. Rival teams established reputations for performing exotic dances, such as the Argentine or Parisian tangos or the Brazilian maxixe. Inspired by the professional teams, amateur couples entered local competitions.

Nonprofessional ballroom dance, meanwhile, extended its reach beyond exclusive ballrooms into public cabarets, roof gardens, and open-air dance halls, further democratizing the tradition. Some members of elite society embraced this expansion of the tradition. Ann Morgan (daughter of financier J. P. Morgan) and Marbury, for instance, sponsored events for young working women that used social dance to promote upward assimilation. However, the further association of these and other venues with the consumption of alcoholic beverages meant that ballroom dance was severely affected by Prohibition in the United States in the 1920s and early '30s. During this era the more solidly established exhibition dance teams focused on vaudeville or film, or they moved to Europe.

This illustration depicts dancers at a restaurant and cabaret in Paris in the early 1900s. Ballroom dancing was popular in the public cabarets and dance halls, where there was an intimate atmosphere and improvisational character to the settings.

Also during this era, the line distinguishing ballroom dance from other sorts of social dance was further blurred, as the primary market for promoting dances moved to the theatre. Ballroom dance events were integrated into the plots of such popular musicals as *No, No, Nanette* (1925) and *Good News* (1927) and into films about contemporary life, such as *Nice People* (1922) and *Our Dancing Daughters* (1928). Moreover, during this time the enormous influence of African American social dance was acknowledged in the ballroom. Steps from the Charleston—introduced in the African American musical *Runnin' Wild* (1923, dance direction by Elida Webb)—moved into the ballroom repertoire, although only a short part of the dance was performed by partners holding hands. [5]

In the 1920s, band arrangements of foxtrots and other ballroom dance music were disseminated through music publishing, recording, and newly networked radio broadcasts. Such exposure ultimately helped establish those dances that have remained standard ballroom fare into the 21st century. Similarly, dance instruction reached an ever-expanding market through franchised studios, such as those of Arthur Murray.

With the end of Prohibition in 1933, ballroom and exhibition ballroom dances further solidified their links with American social life, popular entertainment, and the music industry. The same range of dances was now seen both in public settings and at invitational events, [6] such as country club dances, as well as in popular film sequences set at college dances and country clubs. Popular African American social dances of the first half of the 20th century, such as the lindy, the stomp, and swing dancing, were drawn into the ballroom repertoire, albeit in a somewhat less exuberant form. A few of the best-known public venues for these dances,

# VERNON AND IRENE CASTLE

English dancer Vernon Castle and U.S. dancer Irene Castle were a famous husband-and-wife dance team who added a sense of spontaneity to formal ballroom dancing. They appeared in several vaudeville acts, ran a dance school, and owned two nightclubs in New York City. They originated several dances, including the one-step and the turkey trot.

Vernon Blythe was born on May 2, 1887, in Norwich, Norfolk, England. He went to New York City in 1907 with aspirations of becoming an actor, and soon he was performing comic dances for Lew Fields productions. Irene Foote was born in 1893 in New Rochelle, New York. The couple met in 1910, and Vernon secured a dancing job for her with Fields in the show *The Hen-Pecks*. They married the next year. In 1912 they performed American social dances in Paris at the Café de Paris, and their imaginative choreography and elegant dancing made them a great success. They popularized such dances as the glide, the castle polka, the castle walk, the fox-trot, the hesitation waltz, the maxixe, the tango, and the bunny hug. They were also trendsetters in fashion

*(continued on the next page)*

*(continued from the previous page)*

and hairstyling, Irene being known for her slim figure, bobbed hair, and headbands.

The Castles returned to New York City and performed in the show *The Sunshine Girl* in 1913 before embarking on a nation-wide dancing tour in 1914. Their routines were set to jazz and ragtime beats, which were an instant success with audiences and helped to popularize social dancing in the United States. They wrote *Modern Dancing* in 1914, the same year they performed in *Watch Your Step*, a show set to music by Irving Berlin. The Castles' performing career together was cut short when Vernon enrolled in the British Royal Air Force in 1916. On February 15, 1918, in Fort Worth, Texas, he was killed in an aviation accident during a routine training flight.

Irene continued her theatrical career, starring in the Broadway show *Miss 1917* followed by nearly two dozen movies and a vaudeville act with William Reardon in the early 1920s. However, she never again achieved the wild success she enjoyed while performing with Vernon. Irene compiled letters from Vernon in the book *My Husband* (1919) and later wrote *Castles in the*

*Air* (1958). In 1939 Fred Astaire, who was strongly influenced by the Castles, starred with Ginger Rogers in the motion picture *The Story of Vernon and Irene Castle*. Irene married three more times, taught children's dance classes, and eventually became involved in animal-rescue work. She died on January 25, 1969, in Eureka Springs, Arkansas.

Irene and Vernon Castle perform a ballroom dance in 1914. They popularized dances such as the castle polka and the castle walk, a dance during which the female partner dances backward most of the time.

such as the Savoy and Audubon ballrooms in New York City's Harlem district, survived well into the mid-20th century, often hosting sponsored competitions, such as the preliminary rounds of the Harvest Moon Ball at Madison Square Garden. Meanwhile, the popularity of Caribbean and South American songs and ensembles and the development of Afro-Cuban jazz (early Latin jazz) supported a Latin dance craze, bringing renewed popularity in the 1930s to exhibition teams performing rumba, acrobatic adagio, and slow-dance styles. These professional dance teams also helped promote the Cuban mambo and cha-cha.

# EXHIBITION AND COMPETITIVE BALLROOM DANCE SINCE THE MID-20TH CENTURY

In the second half of the 20th century, social dance genres followed the entertainment industries' pursuit of a youthful audience. Accordingly, popular rock and roll dances (such as the twist), disco dances (such as the hustle), and break dancing were all in turn publicized, dramatized, and commoditized within the ballroom dance context. Older forms of ballroom dance, particularly those derived from 19th-century models, persisted through their association with new sorts of social rituals, most notably those connected with fund-raising. These events, generally called cotillions or debutante balls, served both to raise money for worthy causes and to introduce young people into society. Early ballroom dance styles also continued to be practiced in traditional family settings, such as wedding receptions and Mexican *quinceañera* celebrations, which mark a girl's entry into adulthood.

Exhibition ballroom dance remained popular in Britain and Continental Europe throughout the 20th century, particularly in semi-invitational settings, such as resorts and hotels. Especially after the 1960s, ballroom dance gained a strong following in Asia. Popular interest and scholarly research, moreover, brought new appreciation to both ballroom and social dance as valuable reflections and embodiments of a community's social values. Meanwhile, the regulations governing competitive ballroom dance became more exact as dance teachers switched their focus from inventing new dances to codifying existing ones. Those "official" versions of fox-trots, waltzes, and tangos—all with specified steps, postures, and head positions—have been maintained in European televised competitions and to some degree in Olympic figure skating (specifically in ice dancing).

In the early 21st century, an alternative form of competitive ballroom dance thrived in Europe, North America, and South America in television shows such as *Dancing with the Stars.* These elimination series focused largely on the personalities of the contestants, with individualization earning more points than strict adherence to the rules. Once an expression of elite society, ballroom dance has continued to expand its appeal and adapt its approach in response to the ever-changing aesthetics of contemporary culture.

# TRENDS BEFORE WORLD WAR I

Two trends were evident during the first years of the 20th century, before World War I (1914–18). As if aware of some impending catastrophe, the wealthy society of Europe and the Americas indulged itself to the full in quicker waltzes and faster galops. At the same time, it tried to revive the minuet, gavotte, and pavane, producing only pale and lifeless evocations. There had hardly ever been such a frantic search for new forms, such radical questioning of values previously taken for granted, such a craze among the youth of all nations for individual expression and a more dynamic way of life. All the arts were deeply influenced by the rapid accumulation of discoveries in the physical and social sciences and an increasing awareness of social problems.

Overall, it was an incredibly lively time for dance, which never before had generated so many new ideas or attracted so many people. The ballet was completely rejuvenated under the leadership of Russian impresario Serge Diaghilev (1872–1929). It inspired some of the foremost composers and painters of the day, becoming the primary theatre platform for the most up-to-date work in the arts. Proponents of another reform movement, modern dance, took their cue from the American dancer Isadora Duncan to strike in another way at the artificialities that Romantic ballet had generated. It took vigorous roots in Germany, where its expressionistic forms earned it the name *Ausdruckstanz* ("expressionistic dance"). The ballroom dances were thoroughly revolutionized through infusions of new vitality from South American, Creole, and black sources. With the overwhelming popularity of jazz, the entire spirit and style of social dancing altered radically, becoming vastly more free, relaxed, and intimate through the following decades.

There was also a renewal of interest in the folk dances that had been the expressions of the common people in past centuries. This was fostered partly through special folk-dance societies, partly through various youth movements that saw that these dances might assist in shaping new community feelings. Theatrical dance of all kinds, from the highly stylized, centuries-old dances of Asia to exhibitions of naked female flesh, reached new heights of popularity.

# DIAGHILEV AND HIS ACHIEVEMENTS

The artistic consequences of Diaghilev's Ballets Russes were enormous. Diaghilev's interest in dance began while he was a member of a small circle of intellectuals in St. Petersburg who fought to bring Russia's arts onto the wider European scene. The painters Alexandre Benois and Léon Bakst were his earliest collaborators.

## THE BALLETS RUSSES

The Russian ballet troupe that Diaghilev took to Paris in 1909 boasted some of the best dancers from the imperial theatres in St. Petersburg and Moscow. They set all Paris ablaze. No living person could remember ballets of such quality. For the next 20 years the Ballets Russes, which never appeared in Russia, became the foremost ballet company in the West. Diaghilev, who never choreographed a ballet himself, possessed a singular flair for bringing the right people together. He became the focus of the ballet world, striving for the integration of dance, music, visual design, and libretto into a "total work of art" in which no one element dominated the others.

Between 1909 and 1929, the contributions of many of the finest dancers and choreographers and of some of the most avant-garde, style-setting painters and composers made the Diaghilev company the centre of creative artistic activity. The group became a haven for Russian dancers who emigrated after the 1917 Revolution. It was the first large, permanently travelling company that operated on a private basis and catered to a cosmopolitan Western clientele.

Michel Fokine (1880–1942) was the first choreographer to put Diaghilev's ideas into practice. He worked with contemporary composers, notably the Russian Igor Stravinsky (1882–1971) and the Frenchman Maurice Ravel (1875–1937). Stravinsky composed the score for two of Fokine's best-known ballets, *L'Oiseau de feu* (*The Firebird*; 1910) and *Petrushka* (1911); both are based on old Russian folktales. He drew also upon many eminent composers of the past, such as the Russians Aleksandr Borodin (1833–87) and Nicolay Rimsky-Korsakov (1844–1908), and the Pole Frédéric Chopin (1810–49). His major scenic artists were Benois and Bakst, whose contributions to theatrical design had influences beyond the sphere of ballet. Among his dancers were the Russians Anna Pavlova (1881–1931), who left after the 1909 season to dance with her own company throughout the West as well as Asia, and Vaslav Nijinsky (1890–1950), who succeeded Fokine as the company's choreographer. A classic dancer, Nijinsky was an anticlassic choreographer, specializing in turned-in body movements

Anna Pavlova and Vaslav Nijinsky are photographed in *Le Pavillon d'Armide* ("Armida's Pavillion"), around 1909. Serge Diaghilev's Les Ballets Russes first performed this ballet, which was choreographed by Michel Fokine, in the Mariinsky Theatre in St. Petersburg in 1907. It premiered in Paris in 1909.

and in unusual footwork. In 1912 Nijinsky choreographed *L'Après-midi d'un faune* (*Afternoon of a Faun*) to music written by the French Impressionist composer Claude Debussy (1862–1918)—it is the only Nijinsky ballet still performed. The following year he created *Le Sacre du printemps* (*The Rite of Spring*) to Stravinsky's music. The unconventional ballet was considered scandalous and nearly caused a riot at its Paris premiere.

After Nijinsky's career was cut short by the effects of his mental illness, the dancer Léonide Massine (1896–1979) assumed the role of choreographer. He quickly became noted for his wit and the precisely characterizing gestures of his dancers. His musical collaborators included Stravinsky; Manuel de Falla (1876–1946), whose work was full of the flavour of his native Spain; Ottorino Respighi (1879–1936), noted for his musical evocations of Italian landscapes; and Erik Satie (1866–1925), a Frenchman known for his originality and eccentricity. Massine's designers included leading painters of the School of Paris such as André Derain (1880–1954) and Pablo Picasso (1881–1973). Following Diaghilev's death, Massine created a furor in the 1930s with his ballets based on symphonies by Tchaikovsky and Johannes Brahms. It was considered inappropriate to use symphonic music for dance, and the incorporation of the style and movements of modern dance into the plotless ballets added to the controversy.

Another of Diaghilev's choreographers was Nijinsky's sister, Bronisława Nijinska (1891–1972), who became famous for her massive ensemble groupings, used to great effect in *Les Noces* (*The Wedding*; 1923), and her talent for depicting the follies of contemporary society. Diaghilev's last choreographic discovery was the Russian-trained George Balanchine (1904–83). Balanchine's 1928 ballet, *Apollon Musagète*, was the first of many collaborations with Stravinsky and led the way to the final enthronement of neoclassicism as the dominant choreographic style of the following decades.

## THE CONTINUING TRADITION

When Diaghilev died, his was no longer the only ballet company touring the world. Anna Pavlova's company visited places in Europe, the Americas, Australia, and Asia that had never heard of, let alone seen, ballet. A troupe assembled by Ida Rubinstein (1885–1960) had Nijinska as a choreographer and Stravinsky and Ravel as composers. The Ballets Suédois featured, from 1920 to 1925, another group of avant-garde, largely French and Italian composers, painters, and writers. New dancers came from the schools in Paris, London, and Berlin that were directed by self-exiled Russian teachers. Important developments took place in London, where Dame Marie Rambert

(1888–1982), a Diaghilev dancer, founded the Ballet Rambert, and Ninette de Valois founded the company that became in 1956 the Royal Ballet. In New York, Balanchine set up the School of American Ballet in 1934. From it he drew the dancers for the several companies that led ultimately to the founding of the New York City Ballet in 1948.[2]

## THE SOVIET BALLET

Although Diaghilev's achievements were ignored there, the Soviet Union in the 1920s abounded with the daring choreographic experiments of Fyodor Lopukhov (1886–1973) and others. Despite the official imposition of "socialist realism" as the criterion of artistic acceptability in 1932, ballet gained enormous popularity with the Soviet people. They loved their dancers, who were superbly trained by generations of teachers under the leadership of Agrippina Vaganova (1879–1951).

# MODERN DANCE

Despite the recovery of ballet from its sterility in the late 19th century, other dancers questioned the validity of an art form so inescapably bound to tradition by its relatively limited vocabulary. They wished to change radically the culture con-cept of expressive stage dancing. In a period

of women's emancipation, women stepped to [3]
the front as propagandists for the new dance
and toppled the conventions of the academic
dance. They advocated a dance that arose from
the dancer's innermost impulses to express himself or herself in movement. They took their cues
from music or such other sources as ancient
Greek vase paintings and the dances of Asian
and American Indian cultures.

The pioneers of this new dance were
Isadora Duncan (1877–1927), who stormed
across European stages in her loosely flying
tunic, inspiring a host of disciples and imitators,
and Ruth St. Denis (1877–1968), who surprised
American and European audiences with her
Asian-style dances. With her partner Ted Shawn
(1891–1972) she founded (1915) Denishawn,
which, as a school and performing company,
became the cradle of America's early protag-
onists of modern dance; notable among them
were Martha Graham, Doris Humphrey, and
Charles Weidman. [4]

Duncan believed that ballet technique
distorted the natural movement of the body,
that it "separated the gymnastic movements
of the body completely from the mind," and
that it made dancers move like "articulated
puppets" from the base of the spine. Duncan
worked with simple movements and natural
rhythms, finding her inspiration in the movements of nature—particularly the wind and
waves—as well as in the dance forms that she [5]

Eadweard Muybridge took this photograph between 1884 and 1886 while studying the dancer Isadora Duncan's movement during one of her modern dance pieces. The image appeared as "Woman Dancing" in Muybridge's book *Animal Locomotion* (1887).

had studied in antique sculpture. Elements that were most characteristic of her dancing included lifted, far-flung arm positions, an ecstatically lifted head, unconstrained leaps, strides, and skips, and, above all, strong, flowing rhythms in which one movement melted into the next. Her costumes, too, were unconstrained; she danced barefoot and uncorseted in simple, flowing tunics, with only the simplest props and lighting effects to frame her movements.

Dance, according to Duncan, should be the "divine expression" of the human spirit, and this concern with the inner motivation of dance characterized all early modern choreographers. They presented characters and situations that broke the romantic, fairy-tale surface of contemporary ballet and explored the primitive instincts, the conflicts and passions of man's inner self.

To this end they sought to develop a style of movement that was more natural and more expressive than ballet. Martha Graham, for example, saw the back and, particularly, the pelvis as the centre of all movement, and many of her most characteristic movements originated from a powerful spiral, arch, or curve in the back. Doris Humphrey saw all human movement as a transition between fall (when the body is off balance) and recovery (when it returns to a balanced state), and in many

Martha Graham performs *Strike* in 1928. Graham had left the Denishawn school in 1923, and, in 1927, began to perform more original dances of protest and social comment that she set to avant-garde music.

of her movements the weight of the body was always just off centre, falling and being caught.

Instead of defying gravity, as in ballet, modern dancers emphasized their own weight. Even in their jumps and high extensions, the dancers looked as if they were only momentarily escaping from the downward pull of the Earth, and many of their movements were executed close to or on the floor. Graham developed a wide repertoire of falls, for example, and Mary Wigman's style was characterized by kneeling or crouching, the head often dropped and the arms rarely lifted high into the air.

As ballet sought to conceal or defy the force of gravity, so it also strove to conceal the strain of dancing. Modern dance, on the other hand—particularly the work of Graham—emphasized those qualities. In the jagged phrases, angular limbs, clenched fists, and flexed feet, in the forceful movements of the back and the clear lines of tension running through the movement, Graham's choreography expressed not only the struggle of the dancer against physical limitations but also the power of passion and frustration. Movements were always expressive gestures, never decorative shapes. Often the body and limbs appeared racked and contorted by emotion, for these choreographers, like Nijinsky, were not afraid to appear ugly (as indeed they did to many of their contemporaries).

The structure of early modern dance works responded in part to the fragmented narrative and symbolism characteristic of modernist art and literature. Graham often employed flashback techniques and shifting timescales, as in *Clytemnestra* (1958), or used different dancers to portray different facets of a single character, as in *Seraphic Dialogue* (1955). Groups of dancers formed sculptural wholes, often to represent social or psychological forces, and there was little of the hierarchical division between principals and corps de ballet that operated in ballet.

In the German *Ausdruckstanz* ("expressionistic dance") the central figure was Rudolf Laban (1879–1958), who was more a theoretician and teacher than a choreographer. His researches into the physiological impulses to movement and rhythm crystallized in a formidable system of physical expression. His system of dance notation, known most widely as labanotation, provided the first means for writing down and copyrighting choreographies. His most prolific disciples were Kurt Jooss (1901–79) and Mary Wigman (1886–1973). Jooss became known for his dances containing strong elements of social commentary. Wigman had also studied with Émile Jaques-Dalcroze (1865–1950), who developed eurythmics, a system of movement originally designed to train professional musicians in rhythm. Wigman blended features of both men's techniques into her own new style of dance. When she toured the United States in the 1930s, Americans became aware that they were not alone in their search for new forms of expressive dance. She left behind one of her closest collaborators, Hanya Holm, who became another major figure on the American scene.

Across the United States schools opened, producing small groups of dancers who performed on college campuses and on small stages in the cities. Each choreographer and company brought different materials, artistic points of view, and performing styles to the dance. Perhaps the single element common to all of the many facets of modern dance was the search for new and valid forms of artistic expression.

## MERCE CUNNINGHAM

The Expressionist school dominated modern dance for several decades. From the 1940s onward, however, there was a growing reaction against Expressionism spearheaded by Merce Cunningham (1919–2009). Cunningham wanted to create dance that was about itself—about the kinds of movement of which the human body is capable and about rhythm, phrasing, and structure. Above all, he wanted to create dance that was not subservient to the demands of either narrative or emotional expression. This did not mean that Cunningham wanted to make dance subservient to music or design; on the contrary, though many of his works were collaborations, in the sense that music and design formed a strong part of the total effect, these elements were often conceived—and worked—independently of the actual dance. Cunningham believed that movement should define its own space and set its own rhythms, rather than be influenced by the set and the music. He also felt that it was more interesting and challenging for the spectator to be confronted with these independently functioning elements and then to choose for himself how to relate them to one another.

Believing that all movement was potential dance material, Cunningham developed a style that embraced an extraordinarily wide spectrum, from natural, everyday actions such as sitting down and walking to virtuosic dance movements. Elements of his style even had a close affinity to ballet: jumps tended to be light and airy, the footwork fleet and intricate, and the leg extensions high and controlled. He placed greater emphasis on the vertical and less emphasis on the body's weight and the force of gravity. Like those of Graham, many of Cunningham's movements centred on the back and torso, but they tended less toward dramatic contractions and spirals than toward smaller and more sharply defined tilts, curves, and twists. The arms were frequently held in graceful curves and the feet pointed.

Cunningham's phrases were often composed of elaborate, coordinating movements of the head, feet, body, and limbs in a string of rapidly changing positions. The arrangement of performers on stage was equally complex: at any one moment there might have been several dancers, in what seemed like random groupings, all performing different phrases at the same time. With no main action dominating the stage, the spectator was free to focus on any part of the dance.

While Graham's works were usually structured around the events of a narrative, Cunningham's works usually emerged from the working through of one or more choreographic ideas, whose development (*i.e.*, the ordering of movements into phrases or the number of dancers working at any one time) might then have been determined by chance. Deriving its movements from such formal origins did not mean that Cunningham's works lacked expressive power. One of his pieces, *Winterbranch* (1964), started out as a study based on moving into a space and falling, but it produced a powerful effect on audiences,

Merce Cunningham and Carolyn Brown rehearse Cunningham's ballet *Second Hand* in 1969. The postmodernist ballet had no set decorations and the dancers wore costumes that were designed by American artist Jasper Johns.

who variously interpreted it as a piece about war, concentration camps, or even sea storms. Cunningham believed that the expressive qualities in dance should not be determined by a story line but should simply rise out of movement itself. "The emotion will appear when the movement is danced," he claimed, "because that is where the life is."

## POSTMODERNISM

During the 1960s and '70s a new generation of American choreographers, generally referred to as postmodernist choreographers, took some of Cunningham's ideas even farther. They also believed that ordinary movement could be used in dance, but they rejected the strong element of virtuosity in Cunningham's technique and the complexities of his phrasing and structure, insisting that such a style interfered with the process of seeing and feeling the movement clearly. Consequently, the postmodernists replaced conventional dance steps with simple movements such as rolling, walking, skipping, and running. Their works concentrated on the basic principles of dance: space, time, and the weight and energy of the dancer's body.

Postmodernists discarded spectacle as another distraction from the real business of movement. Costumes were often ordinary practice or street clothes, there was little or no set and lighting, and many performances took place in lofts, galleries, or out-of-doors. Narrative and expression were discarded, and the dance structures were usually very simple, involving either the repetition and accumulation of simple phrases or the working through of simple movement games or tasks. In Tom Johnson's *Running Out of Breath* (1976) the dancer simply ran around the stage reciting a text until he ran out of breath.

Most avant-garde modern-dance companies have been quite small and have occupied a position on the fringe of the dance world, attracting only small and specialist audiences. Although mainstream modern dance now attracts large audiences in both Europe and North America, it too was for many decades a minority art form, often playing to only a handful of spectators. Modern-dance companies were then, and still are, relatively small. Partly because they lack funding, they tend to use less elaborate costume and staging, and they perform in small theatres where contact with the audience is close.

## NEW RHYTHMS, NEW FORMS IN THE 1900S

The changes in the social climate that were evident in the 20th century had a notable influence on the ballrooms.

# LATIN AMERICAN AND JAZZ DANCES

The younger generation in Europe eagerly took up the more vivacious, dynamic, and passionate social dances from the New World. The turning dances of the 19th century gave way to such walking dances as the two-step, the one-step, or turkey trot, the fox-trot, and the quickstep, performed to the new jagged rhythms. These rhythms were African in origin, whether from the Latin American tangos and rumbas or from the African American jazz.

Jazz dance—any dance to jazz accompaniments, composed of a profusion of forms—paralleled the birth and spread of jazz itself from roots in black American society and was popularized in ballrooms by the big bands of the swing era (1930s and '40s). It radically altered the style of American and European stage and social dance in the 20th century. The term is sometimes used more narrowly to describe (1) popular stage dance (except tap dance) and (2) jazz-derived or jazz-influenced forms of modern dance. It excludes social dances lacking jazz accompaniment—e.g., the rumba and other Latin American dances.

Jazz dance developed from both 19th- and 20th-century stage dance and traditional black social dances and their white ballroom offshoots. On the stage, minstrel show performers in the 19th century developed tap dancing

A jazz dancer performs an athletic move during the 1950s. Jazz dance paralleled the birth and spread of jazz music from roots in black American society and was popularized in ballrooms by the big bands of the swing era.

from a combination of Irish jigging, English clog dancing, and African rhythmic stamping. Tap dance and such social dances as the cakewalk and shuffle became popular vaudeville acts and appeared in Broadway revues and musical comedies as these replaced vaudeville early in the 20th century. In addition, comedy, specialty, and character dances to jazz rhythms became standard stage routines. By the 1940s elements of jazz dance had appeared in modern dance and in motion picture choreography.

Although the stage popularized certain social dances, many others were transmitted mainly in social gatherings. The dances that gave rise to social forms of jazz dance developed from rural slave dances. In both early dances and 20th-century jazz dances, there is a noticeable continuity of dance elements and motions. The eagle rock and the slow drag (late 19th century) as well as the Charleston and the jitterbug have elements in common with certain Caribbean and African dances. In addition, the slow drag contributed to the fish of the 1950s; the ring shout, which survived from the 18th into the 20th century, in isolated areas, influenced the cakewalk.

About 1900 the cakewalk, popularized through stage shows, became a craze in European and American ballrooms. In its wake appeared other social dances such as the Charleston (1920s), the jitterbug (1930s and '40s), the twist (1960s), and disco dancing (1970s). Some, like the fox-trot, borrowed European dance steps and fitted them to jazz rhythms. The growth of radio, television, and recording, which popularized black music among wide audiences, greatly aided the diffusion of these dances. Fusing ballet with jazz has led in recent years to the formation of such troupes as Canada's Les Ballets Jazz de Montreal (founded 1972).

## DANCE CONTESTS AND CODES

After 1912, when ballroom tango became the rage of the dancing world, even elegant hotels invited their clientele to their "tango teas." In fashionable restaurants professional dance couples demonstrated the new styles. In 1892 New York City saw one of the first cakewalk competitions, and in 1907 Nice advertised the first tango contest. After the first world dance competition in 1909, in Paris, this became an annual event, which in 1913 lasted for two weeks. But it was England that acted as arbiter of taste for the new movements in social dance. There the first dance clubs, like the Keen Dancers' Society (later the Boston Club), were founded in 1903. In 1904 the Imperial Society of Teachers of Dancing was established, and in 1910 the periodical *Dancing Times* made its bow. After World War I the English version of the fox-trot was acknowledged as the essence of the internationally acclaimed "English style." Victor Silvester's *Modern Ballroom Dancing* (1928) became the handbook of the dancing world until it was succeeded by Alex Moore's *Ballroom Dancing* (1936). The English style involved strict definitions for the five standard dances—quickstep, waltz, fox-trot, tango, and blues—to which were added after 1945 the Latin American rumba, samba, calypso, and cha-cha. What was left of the social barriers existing in 1900 between the exclusive and the popular dancing establishments was swept away.

Many observers were indignant about the changes taking place. Even so liberal a historian as Curt Sachs could not refrain from stating:

> Since the Brazilian maxixe of 1890 and the cakewalk of 1903 broke up the pattern of turns and glides that dominated the European round dances, our generation has adopted with disquieting rapidity a succession of Central American dances, in an effort to replace what has been lost to modern Europe: multiplicity, power, and expressiveness of movement to the point of grotesque distortion of the entire body. ...All [of these dances are] compressed into even movement, all emphasizing strongly the erotic element, and all in that glittering rhythm of syncopated four-four measures classified as ragtime. (From Curt Sachs, op. cit., pp. 444–445.)

Sachs went on to note the rapid rise and fall in popularity of individual dances and suggested an impermanence to the entire movement.

# EFFECT ON FOLK DANCING

As social dancing spread with the advent of the radio and the phonograph, the regions where genuine folk dancing was practiced became fewer. It continued least corrupted by the new forms in those countries outside the mainstream of Western urbanization and industrialization. Spain maintained its vigorous tradition of flamenco dancing, and in Hungary the composers Béla Bartók (1881–1945) and Zoltán Kodály (1882–1967) collected the remnants of a wealth of folk song and dance folklore. Minority groups such as the Basques in Spain did likewise to maintain their identity against the overpowering influences of their neighbours.

Folk dancing remained a vital reality in the Soviet Union, especially in those European and Asiatic provinces that had distinctive ethnic populations and were far removed from Moscow, Leningrad, and other centres with Western contacts. In the industrial nations of Europe and the Americas, special nationwide councils and societies were founded to preserve the traditional folk dance that was under threat of extinction.

# EXPERIMENTS

Technological progress itself became the subject of dance and dancing. In the Soviet Union, there were experiments during the

1920s with dances created to express urban traffic, the accuracy of machine work, and the grandeur of skyscrapers. In Germany, the painter Oskar Schlemmer (1888–1943) realized his vision of a dance of pure, geometric form in the *Triadisches Ballet* performed in Stuttgart in 1922. In 1926 a sound vision of the technological ages, *Ballet mécanique* (*Mechanical Ballet*), by the American composer George Antheil (1900–59), was scored for mechanical pianos, automobile horns, electric bells, and airplane propellers. It was written not for the live dancer but for an animated film.

# TAP

Tap is the style of dance in which a dancer wearing shoes fitted with heel and toe taps sounds out audible beats by rhythmically striking the floor or any other hard surface. Tap originated in the United States through the fusion of several ethnic percussive dances, primarily African tribal dances and Scottish, Irish, and English clog dances, hornpipes, and jigs. Until the last few decades of the 20th century, it was believed that African slaves and Irish indentured servants had observed each other's dances on Southern plantations and that tap dancing was born from this contact. In the late 20th century, however, researchers suggested that tap instead was nurtured in such urban environments as the Five

Points District in New York City, where a variety of ethnic groups lived side by side under crowded conditions and in constant contact with the distinctly urban rhythms and syncopations of the machine age.

In the mid- to late 1800s, dance competitions were a common form of entertainment. Later called cutting contests, these intense challenges between dancers were an excellent breeding ground for new talent. Dancers matured by learning each other's techniques and rhythmic innovations. The primary showcase for tap of this era was the minstrel show, which was at its peak from approximately 1850 to 1870.

During the following decades, styles of tap dancing evolved and merged. Among the ingredients that went into the mix were buck dancing (a dance similar to but older than the clog dance), soft-shoe dancing (a relaxed, graceful dance done in soft-soled shoes and made popular in vaudeville), and buck-and-wing dancing (a fast and flashy dance usually done in wooden-soled shoes and combining Irish clogging styles, high kicks, and complex African rhythms and steps such as the shuffle and slide; it is the forerunner of rhythm tap). Tap dance as it is known today did not emerge until roughly the 1920s, when "taps," nailed or screwed onto shoe soles at the toes and heels, became popular. During this time entire chorus lines in shows such as *Shuffle Along* (1921) first appeared on stage with "tap shoes," and the dance they did became known as tap dancing.

Tap dance was a particularly dynamic art form, and dancers continually molded and shaped it. Dancers such as Harland Dixon and Jimmy Doyle (a duo known for their buck-and-wing dancing) impressed audiences and influenced developing dancers with their skill, ingenuity, and creativity. In addition to shaping dance performance, tap dancers influenced the evolution of popular American music in the early to mid-20th century; drummers in particular drew ideas as well as inspiration from the dancers' rhythmic patterns and innovations. Early recordings of tap dancers demonstrate that their syncopations were actually years ahead of the rhythms in popular music. 4 5

## VAUDEVILLE

In the early 20th century, vaudeville variety shows moved to the entertainment forefront, and tap dancers such as Greenlee and Drayton, Pat Rooney, Sr., and George White traveled the country. A number of family acts formed, including that of the future Broadway actor, producer, and songwriter George M. Cohan, who with his sister, mother, and father formed the Four Cohans. The Covan brothers together with their wives formed the Four Covans, one of the most sensational fast tap acts ever. The comedian and dancer Eddie Foy, Sr.,

The legendary tap dancer Bill "Bojangles" Robinson performs with his shadow on a New York stage in 1941. A top vaudeville star and acclaimed performer in motion pictures, Robinson invented many new steps, including the "stair dance," and amazed dancers with his ability to run backward almost as fast as other people could run forward.

appeared with his seven tap-dancing children, the Seven Little Foys. By the late 1910s, more than 300 theatres around the country hosted vaudeville acts.

According to the producer Leonard Reed, throughout the 1920s "there wasn't a show that didn't feature tap dancing. If you couldn't dance, you couldn't get a job!" Nightclubs, vaudeville, and musicals all featured tap dancers, whose names often appeared on the many marquees that illuminated New York's Broadway. Stars of the day, including Fred Astaire and his sister, Adele, brought yet more light to the "Great White Way" with their elegant dancing. Bill "Bojangles" Robinson, known for dancing on the balls of his feet (the toe taps) and for his exquisite "stair dance," was the first black tap dancer to break through the Broadway colour line, becoming one the best-loved and highest-paid performers of his day.

Because this was an era when tap dancing was a common skill among performers, a tap dancer had to create something unique to be noticed. The Berry Brothers' act, for example, included rhythmic, synchronized cane twirling and dazzling acrobatics. Cook and Brown had one of the finest knockabout acts. King, King, and King danced in convict outfits, chained together doing close-to-the-floor fast tap work. Buster West tap-danced in "slap shoes"— oversized clown-style shoes that, because of their extended length, slapped audibly on the floor during a routine—and did break dancing decades before it had a name. Will Mahoney tap-danced on a giant xylophone.

The "challenge"—in which tap dancers challenged one another to a dancing "duel"—had been a major part of the tap dancer's education from the beginning. It filtered into many theatrical acts. Possibly the finest exponents of the challenge were the Four Step Brothers, whose act consisted of furious, flying steps, then a moment when each attempted to top the others.

From the outset, tap dancers have stretched the art form, dancing to a wide variety of music and improvising new styles. Among these innovative styles were flash (dance movements that incorporated acrobatics and were often used to finish a dance); novelty (the incorporation into a routine of specialty props, such as jump ropes, suitcases, and stairs); eccentric, legomania, and comedy (each of which used the body in eccentric and comic ways to fool the eye and characteristically involved wild and wiggly leg movements); swing tap, also known as classical tap (combining the upper body movement found in 20th-century ballet and jazz with percussive, syncopated footwork, a style used extensively in the movies); class (precision dancing performed by impeccably dressed dancers); military (the use of military marching and drum rhythms); and rhythm, close floor, and paddle and roll (each of which emphasized footwork using heel and toe taps, typically of a rapid and rhythmic nature).

For each one of these styles there were hundreds of dancers creating a unique version. John Bubbles, for instance, has gone down in history as the "Father of Rhythm Tap." Though he may not have been the very first tap dancer to use the heel tap to push rhythm from the 1920s jazz beat to the 1930s swing beat, he certainly was the most influential; generations of dancers learned his style. Three young dancers from Philadelphia—the Condos Brothers (Frank, Nick, and Steve)—became legendary among dancers for their exceptionally fast, rhythmic footwork; few tap dancers ever achieved Nick's mastery of a difficult move he is credited with inventing known as the five-tap wing. Of the eccentric and legomania dancers, Buddy Ebsen, Henry ("Rubber Legs") Williams, and Hal Leroy stand out. A unique style was invented by one of tap's greatest dancers, Clayton ("Peg Leg") Bates. After losing his leg at age 12, he reinvented tap to fit his own specifications—a peg and a shoe with two taps.

## NIGHTCLUBS

From the 1920s to the '40s, fans of tap could find their favourite dancers in a new venue, nightclubs, where—together with singers and bands—dancers became regular features. A single evening's show could involve as many as 20 tap dancers—a featured solo dancer, a featured duo or trio act, and a chorus line. This formula was common across the nation in venues such as the Cotton Club (Harlem, New York City), the Plantation Club (Culver City, California), the Cocoanut Grove (Los Angeles), and Ciro's (Hollywood). Many tap dance luminaries, including Ruby Keeler, the Nicholas Brothers, and Louis DaPron, began their careers in nightclubs.

Nightclubs and other live shows (vaudeville, Broadway) were segregated in the early years. The white circuit included such prestigious routes as the Orpheum circuit and such acts as that of Fred and Adele Astaire. African American artists, however, generally relied on the Theatre Owners' Booking Association (TOBA), which booked black entertainers in the "chitlin circuit" (venues that catered to black audiences); TOBA nurtured such performers as Leonard Reed and Willie Bryant, creators of the Shim Sham Shimmy (c. 1927; the "national anthem of tap"), and the Whitman Sisters. The "Chop Suey circuit" of Chinese nightclubs—primarily in San Francisco and New York City—featured artists such as Toy and Wing (Dorothy Takahashi Toy and Paul Wing) and catered mainly to white tourists and military men and women.

With the help of a few open-minded booking agents, African American entertainers eventually broke the colour line by sheer determination and skill. Bill Robinson is credited with being the first African American solo entertainer to perform in big-time vaudeville shows. Others soon followed, and shows had begun to be integrated by the 1930s and '40s, but not until the 1970s had performance opportunities noticeably improved.

## FILM

An entirely new arena for tap dancers opened up with the introduction of "talking" motion pictures. Although the technology for sound on film had been around for several years, it was not until *The Jazz Singer* (1927) that the public accepted this new medium. The advent of sound enabled entire acts of many popular vaudeville tap dancers to be captured on film. Some dancers who had been Broadway stars—including Bill Robinson, Fred Astaire, Eleanor Powell, and Ginger Rogers—found a new stardom in Hollywood in the early 1930s. They extended the possibilities of tap once more by creating entirely new material specifically intended for film. The first tap dance numbers on film had been shot straight on, with little or no camera movement (early sound cameras were stationary until Dorothy Arzner created the boom mike). The early dance numbers also typically used cutaways from the dancers to actors or featured close-ups on the dancers' faces or feet. Working closely with directors and cinematographers, Fred Astaire was the first major film dancer to insist that there be few,

Ginger Rogers and Fred Astaire tap dance during a number for the musical comedy film *Swing Time* (1936). The movie was the fifth teaming of Rogers and Astaire. Astaire, who choreographed the dance numbers, did not believe in improvisation and painstakingly planned out key sequences in the minutest detail.

if any, cutaways and that the camera follow him, head to toe, throughout his numbers. He set the standard for how tap dance was shot during the next three decades.

In 1934 a young dancer, six-year-old Shirley Temple, took the film world by storm and became the country's top box-office draw from 1935 to 1938. Between 1934 and 1940 she made 24 films and arguably did more for tap dance's popularity than any single person in the dance's history. Despite the Great Depression, enrollment soared at tap dance schools throughout the country.

From the 1930s to the early 1950s, musical films and stage shows served to distract the public from bleak social conditions brought on by events such as the Great Depression and World War II. Every major studio featured tap dancers: among others, MGM had Gene Kelly and Vera-Ellen; Warner Brothers had Ruby Keeler and Gene Nelson; Twentieth Century-Fox had the Nicholas Brothers, Dan Dailey, and Betty Grable; and Universal Studios had Peggy Ryan and the Jivin' Jacks and Jills. Ann Miller and Donald O'Connor worked for several studios. Outstanding tap dancers, such as Hermes Pan, Willie Covan, Louis DaPron, Miriam Nelson, Nick Castle, Buddy Bradley, and Henry LeTang, were hired to choreograph musical sequences.

Although black artists of all types were prevented from starring in mainstream feature films during this time, many dancers nonetheless appeared as specialty acts in feature films, musical short subjects, and Soundies (three-minute black-and-white sound films that could be viewed on coin-operated 16-mm rear-projection machines called Panorams in restaurants, bars, and other public places). The artistry of a vast array of African American talent—among these Buck and Bubbles, Jeni LeGon, and Tip Tap and Toe—can be seen in three-minute celluloid flashes. Even the exceptional Asian American dance team Toy and Wing can be seen as a specialty act in *Deviled Ham* (1937).

Though vaudeville was on the wane by the mid-1930s and dead by the 1940s, tap dancers continued to be popular acts in nightclubs and musical shows. Paul Draper and Georgie Tapps were the first to popularize tap-dancing to classical music, and they performed at such glamorous nightclubs as Manhattan's Rainbow Room. Throughout the Big Band era, tap dancers performed with well-known orchestras; Bunny Briggs, for example, danced with the bands of Duke Ellington, Earl Hines, and others, and Ralph Brown was featured with Count Basie, Dizzy Gillespie, and Charlie Parker, among others.

The popularity of tap dancing began to decline in the 1950s. This change is often attributed to a series of events in the 1940s. In 1942 Agnes de Mille introduced narrative ballet into the Broadway show with *Oklahoma!*

Although in *Rodeo* (1942) she had also been the first to introduce tap dance into ballet, her billing as a choreographer and the false competition with ballet made tap seem "hokey" and passé. Another factor in the waning of tap dance was a dramatic drop in nightclub attendance, as men and women who had come home from service overseas concentrated on getting an education, starting careers, and raising families.

## TELEVISION AND LAS VEGAS

The introduction of television and the rise of Las Vegas, Nevada, as a popular tourist attraction saved tap dance from a slow death. Variety shows, which included tap dancers along with their other acts, were among the most popular programs in the early decades of television, including *The Colgate Comedy Hour, Your Show of Shows, The Milton Berle Show,* and *The Ed Sullivan Show,* to name but a few. For many tap dancers, television presented a new challenge. Most tap acts had subsisted on one surefire three-to-eight-minute act, which they had performed for their entire career. In live theatre this had not posed a problem, because they rarely, if ever, appeared more than once a year before the same regional audience. When the act was broadcast on television, however, the entire nation saw it, and the dancers were compelled to create new routines to keep their acts fresh. Most—including black tap acts, such as Peg Leg Bates, who had been confined to the black vaudeville circuit until the age of television—met the challenge and were able to make the transition to television. Starting in the 1950s, tap dancers also found new opportunities for appearing onstage in Las Vegas, which had developed into an entertainment resort. Many older tap dancers retired there and spent their final performing years in casino showrooms.

Despite its adaptation to a new medium and new venues, tap dance was struggling to survive. Starting in the 1970s, several tap companies were formed, and, in an effort to court a younger audience, they traveled on the college circuit. The first of these were the Jazz Tap Ensemble (founded 1979 by Lynn Dally), Rhapsody in Taps (cofounded 1981 by Linda Sohl-Donnell and Toni Relin), and the American Tap Dance Foundation (founded 1986 as the American Tap Dance Orchestra by Brenda Bufalino, Tony Waag, and Honi Coles).

## REBIRTH

A slow resurgence began in the 1980s, when successful Broadway shows such as *42nd Street* (opened 1980) and *Black and Blue* (opened 1989) prominently featured tap. But only with the emergence of the dancer, musician, and actor Gregory Hines did tap secure a place in the late 20th century. He bolstered his dynamic, masculine style with a definite preference for modern rather than nostalgic music. In the film *Tap* (1989), he updated the image of tap and brought a new style of tap dancing to the public.

In 1984 the dazzling 10-year-old Savion Glover took over the title role of the Broadway show *The Tap Dance Kid*. The public, as well as many veterans of tap, were impressed by his extremely fast and precise footwork. As he grew into his late teens and early twenties, Glover developed his own distinct style, which he called free-form hard core, rooted in the rhythms of funk and hip-hop. Not only did he star in the award-winning *Bring in 'da Noise, Bring in 'da Funk* (1996), but he won a Tony Award for his choreography. As he matured, he continued to improvise and experiment while acknowledging a debt to the past masters of tap. The style and innovation of artists such as Glover made tap appealing to a new generation at the dawn of a new century. Tap, which in the 1970s had seemed a dying art, emerged in some ways stronger than ever. To be sure, this was thanks at least in part to the people who formed tap dance companies that would keep tap alive and to those who researched the history of tap dance.

# SAVION GLOVER

American dancer and choreographer Savion Glover, born on November 19, 1973, in Newark, New Jersey, became known for his unique pounding style of tap dancing, called hitting. He brought renewed interest in dance, particularly among youths and minorities.

As a young child, Glover displayed an affinity for rhythms, and at age four he began taking drumming lessons. Deemed too advanced for the class, however, he then enrolled at the Newark Community School of the Arts and soon became the youngest person in the school's history to receive a full scholarship. At age seven he began taking tap lessons and quickly developed a passion for rhythm tap, a form that uses all parts of the foot to create sound. His talent attracted the attention of a choreographer for the Broadway musical *The Tap Dance Kid*, and Glover served as an understudy before taking the lead role in 1984. He returned to Broadway in 1989, performing in the musical revue *Black and Blue*, and was nominated for a Tony Award. A role in the motion picture *Tap* (1989) followed. Glover, who had long made a point of learning as much as he could from old tap masters, soon began teaching tap classes. He also developed his own tap style, which he

*(continued on the next page)*

*(continued from the previous page)*

christened free-form hard core, while working with dancers such as Gregory Hines, Henry LeTang, and Sammy Davis, Jr.

In 1990 Glover created his first choreography, for a festival at New York City's Apollo Theater. Two years later he became the youngest-ever recipient of a National Endowment for the Arts grant. He portrayed a young Jelly Roll Morton in the musical *Jelly's Last Jam*, which debuted in Los Angeles in 1991 before opening on Broadway the following year and touring in 1994. In 1995 *Bring in 'Da Noise, Bring in 'Da Funk* opened off broadway. Glover choreographed and starred in the musical, which featured a series of vignettes that chronicled African American history. A huge success, the show soon moved to Broadway, and in 1996 it won four Tony Awards, including a best choreographer award for Glover.

His numerous other appearances included a regular role (1990–95) on the children's television show *Sesame Street*. In 2000 Glover appeared in director Spike Lee's film *Bamboozled* and in 2001 made an appearance in *Bojangles*, a television biopic of tap dancer Bill "Bojangles" Robinson starring Hines. He premiered *Classical Savion*, a production that featured him tapping to classical music, in New York City in 2005; the show later toured the United States. In 2006 Glover choreographed the tap dances performed by the penguin Mumble in the computer-animated *Happy Feet.* That year he also formed his own production company, which oversaw his HooFeRzCLuB School for Tap and produced later shows, including *Sole Power* (2010) and *Om* (2014).

In 2015 the *New York Times* announced the return of Glover to Broadway in a collaboration with singer and actor Audra McDonald and director George C. Wolfe in the musical *Shuffle Along, or the Making of the Musical Sensation of 1921 and All That Followed.* Glover choreographed the musical, which is based on the 1921 production of *Shuffle Along,* the first all-black Broadway show.

# DANCE SINCE 1945

Dance of all kinds emerged from World War II, more vital and more expansive than before.

## SOCIAL DANCE

Postwar social dancing was marked by continuing exuberance and enthusiasm. Dances such as the jitterbug, popular throughout the 1930s and '40s, included lively turns and lifts with rapid footwork. Motion pictures and television helped to spread such rock and roll dances as the twist more rapidly and widely than dances had travelled before. A characteristic of this new generation of jazz-based dances was the lack of bodily contact between the participants, who vibrated their legs, gesticulated with their hands, swung their shoulders, and twitched their heads.

Many observers attempted to draw social implications of all kinds from these dances, which began to spread also among the youth of the Communist countries of Eastern Europe and Asia. Among the more interesting interpretations was that of Frances Rust:

> ... this type of dancing can be thought of as "progression" rather than "regression." Historically speaking, country-dancing of a communal or group nature gives way, with the break up of communities, to partnered-up ballroom dancing with a concentration on couples rather than groups. This, in turn, is now replaced amongst young people by partner-less dancing, which, although individualistic, seems none-the-less, to be rooted in a striving for community feeling and group solidarity (from *Dance in Society*; Routledge and Kegon Paul, 1969).

In the mid-1970s, disco dancing brought a return to dancing with a partner in choreographed steps in dances such as the hustle and the bump. Disco was influenced by modern jazz dancing and became rather athletic, incorporating kicks, turns, and even backflips. Athletic dance moves continued to develop, especially in the 1980s in break dancing, an acrobatic style that featured intricate contortions, mime-like walking moves, and rapid spins on the neck and shoulders. Less complicated dance styles also were found, such as slam dancing, in which the dancers hurled their bodies against each other's, and dances such as the pogo, in which dancers jumped in place to the music's rhythm. Partner dancing never disappeared completely, however, and was especially prominent in the "western-swing" dancing of American country and western music.

## DANCE IN THE THEATRE

On the postwar ballet scene there were no revolutionary developments such as those of Diaghilev earlier in the century. The classical ballet style reigned supreme throughout the West and in the Soviet Union. The leading Russian companies, the Bolshoi Ballet in Moscow and the Kirov Ballet in St. Petersburg, continued the great 19th-century Russian tradition of full-length dramatic ballets.

# JEROME ROBBINS

Jerome Robbins, whose original surname was Rabinowitz, was born on October 11, 1918, in New York City. Robbins is considered one of the most popular and imaginative American choreographers of the 20th century. Robbins was first known for his skillful use of contemporary American themes in ballets and Broadway and Hollywood musicals. He won acclaim for highly innovative ballets structured within the traditional framework of classical dance movements.

The son of Russian-Jewish immigrants, Rabinowitz studied chemistry for one year at New York University before embarking on a career as a dancer in 1936. He studied a wide array of dance traditions, appeared with the Gluck Sandor–Felicia Sorel Dance Center, and danced in the chorus of several Broadway musicals. In 1940 he joined Ballet Theater (now American Ballet Theatre), where he soon began dancing such important roles as Petrouchka. (About this time he and his parents changed the family name to Robbins.) In 1944 Robbins choreographed his first, spectacularly successful ballet, *Fancy Free*, with a musical score by the young composer Leonard Bernstein. This ballet, featuring three American sailors on shore leave in New York City during World War II, displayed Robbins's acute sense of theatre and his ability to capture the essence of contemporary American dance using the vocabulary of classical ballet. Later that year Robbins and Bernstein, in collaboration with the lyricists Betty Comden and Adolph Green, expanded *Fancy Free* into a successful Broadway musical called *On the Town.*

For the next phase of his career Robbins was to divide his time between musicals and ballet. He created such ballets as *Interplay* (1945) and *Facsimile* (1946). In 1948 Robbins joined the newly founded New York City Ballet (NYCB) as both dancer and choreographer, and the following year he became its associate artistic director under George Balanchine. Robbins created many important ballets for NYCB, some of the earliest being *The Cage* (1951), *Afternoon of a Faun* (1953), and *The Concert* (1956). These innovative works display his gift for capturing the essence of a particular era through his mastery of vernacular dance styles and his understanding of gesture.

*(continued on the next page)*

*(continued from the previous page)*

For the Broadway stage, Robbins choreographed a string of musicals, including *Billion Dollar Baby* (1946), *High Button Shoes* (1947), and *Look Ma, I'm Dancin'* (1948). Robbins won the Antoinette Perry (Tony) Award for best choreographer in 1948 for *High Button Shoes.* He also created the dance sequences for the musicals *Call Me Madam* (1950), Rodgers and Hammerstein's *The King and I* (1951), and *The Pajama Game* (1954); and he adapted, choreographed, and directed a musical version of *Peter Pan* (1954) that was subsequently adapted for television in 1955 and for which Robbins won an Emmy Award.

His Broadway career is well represented by *West Side Story* (1957), a musical that transplants the tragic story of Romeo and Juliet to the gritty milieu of rival street gangs in New York City. Robbins conceived, directed, and choreographed this work, which featured a musical score by Bernstein, lyrics by Stephen Sondheim, and set designs by Robbins's longtime collaborator Oliver Smith. *West Side Story* was immediately recognized as a major achievement in the history of American musical theatre,

American dancer, choreographer, and director Jerome Robbins demonstrates a dance move to actor George Chakiris (*left*), who plays the Sharks' gang leader Bernardo, during the filming of *West Side Story* in 1961. *West Side Story* was recognized as an outstanding achievement in the history of the American musical theatre and the film adaptation was considered one of the greatest of all time.

**with its innovative setting, electric pacing, and tense, volatile dance sequences. Robbins received the 1958 Tony Award for best choreography for the Broadway version and Academy Awards for his choreography and codirection (with Robert Wise) of the highly successful 1961 film version. (The original**

*(continued on the next page)*

*(continued from the previous page)*

musical was successfully revived on Broadway in **1980** and **2009**.) He directed and choreographed the popular musical *Gypsy* in **1959** and the even more successful *Fiddler on the Roof* in **1964**.

It was after *Fiddler on the Roof* that Robbins turned his attention more exclusively to the ballet. Since **1958** Robbins had worked with the ballet company he had founded, Ballets U.S.A., which toured sporadically until **1961**. In **1965** Robbins resumed creating ballets with his acclaimed *Les Noces*. For the next three years he worked on an experimental theatre project, the American Theatre Laboratory, but in **1969** he returned to NYCB. He was a resident choreographer and a ballet master there until **1983**, when he and Peter Martins became ballet masters in chief (codirectors) of the company shortly before Balanchine's death. Robbins continued to write ballets for NYCB, including *Dances at a Gathering* (**1969**); *The Goldberg Variations* (**1971**); *Requiem Canticles* (**1972**); *In G Major* (**1975**); *Glass Pieces*, performed to the music of Phillip Glass (**1983**); *In Memory of...* (**1985**); *Ives, Songs* (**1988**); and *West Side Story Suite* (**1995**). Many of his later ballets are more classical in style and more abstract in subject matter than his earlier works.

Robbins's *Broadway*, a compilation of excerpts from 11 Broadway musicals that Robbins had directed or choreographed, opened on Broadway in 1989. Robbins resigned as codirector of NYCB in 1990, though he continued to choreograph for the company. His last work, *Brandenburg*, premiered there in 1997. Robbins died in New York City on July 29, 1998.

In 1958 Robbins formed a charitable organization bearing his name, the Jerome Robbins Foundation. Originally intended to fund dance and theatre projects, the foundation also provided financial support to projects combating the effects of the AIDS crisis. In accordance with Robbins's earlier wishes, in 2003 the foundation awarded the first Jerome Robbins Prizes in recognition of excellence in dance.

The popularity of ballet and the establishment of many apparently permanent companies made inevitable wide variations in style and content. International tours were resumed on a large scale. There was also considerable interaction in terms of style and personnel between ballet and modern dance. This was especially true at the New York City Ballet, founded in the late 1940s by George Balanchine and Lincoln Kirstein. The company presented many new works by choreographers such as Jerome Robbins, William Dollar, and Sir Frederick Ashton (the latter principal choreographer and director of Britain's Royal Ballet), but it was Balanchine's style that dominated the company through great ballets such as *The Nutcracker* (1954) and *Don Quixote* (1965) and more abstract works such as *Agon* (1957) and *Jewels* (1967). After Balanchine's death in 1983, Robbins and dancer-choreographer Peter Martins became ballet masters in chief and continued the company's tradition and at the same time introduced new works.

Another leading company was the American Ballet Theatre, founded in 1939. Its repertoire combined a broad range of works by choreographers such as Antony Tudor and Eliot Feld and balanced classical ballets with established contemporary pieces and newly commissioned works. After the retirement of codirectors Lucia Chase and Oliver Smith in 1980, the great Latvian-born U.S. dancer Mikhail Baryshnikov was named artistic director.

The development of modern dance continued in the work of innovative dancer-choreographers who formed their own companies to explore new styles of dance. Martha Graham's expressive dance centred on mythic and legendary themes, whether ancient, as in *Primitive Mysteries* (1931) and *Clytemnestra* (1958), or modern, as in *Appalachian Spring* (1944). One of Graham's dancers, Merce Cunningham, concentrated on abstract movement that

Choreographer Twyla Tharp and dancer Mikhail Baryshnikov rehearse a dance production for the American Ballet Theatre (ABT) in 1975. Baryshnikov served as the artistic director of the ABT from 1980 to 1989. In 1988 Tharp disbanded her company and joined the ABT, where she was artistic associate until 1990.

minimized emotional content and experimented with techniques for achieving purity of movement, including arranging sequences of dance steps by flipping a coin. Twyla Tharp was another experimental choreographer whose early work reduced dance to its most fundamental level—movement through open areas, often without music. Her later work melded classical ballet and jazz with modern dance. A different perspective was offered by Arthur Mitchell, who left the New York City Ballet to found the Dance Theatre of Harlem, a company with strong roots in classical ballet.

The American musical theatre benefitted from the techniques of theatrical dance forms. Choreographers of ballet and modern dance also created works for musical comedy. Agnes de Mille choreographed *Rodeo* (1942) for the Ballet Russe de Monte Carlo and later created many modern works for the American Ballet Theatre; she also choreographed the stage and film versions of Rodgers and Hammerstein's *Oklahoma!* (1943 and 1955, respectively) and the stage versions of *Carousel* (1945) and *Paint Your Wagon* (1951). Jerome Robbins contributed excellent works for the stage in *The King and I* (1951) and *Fiddler on the Roof* (1967), as well as the stage and film versions of *West Side Story* (1957 and 1961).

Companies presenting dances from India, Sri Lanka, Bali, and Thailand were no longer considered exotic on Western stages, and their influences contributed to both ballet and modern dance. Numerous ensembles sprang up, their repertoires based on traditional national dances adapted for the stage. Many were modelled on the Moiseyev folk-dance company of the Soviet Union, which had attracted large audiences during its frequent European and American tours. Similar companies existed in several eastern European countries, in Israel, and in some African nations, as well as in Brazil, Mexico, and the Philippines.

From the beginning of the 20th century, the dance scene became extremely multifaceted and colourful. If some of its manifestations appeared contradictory, that could be regarded as proof of its vitality. No other century granted dance so prominent a role among its social activities. Indications of this prominence included a vast increase in dance research and writing, the opening of colleges and universities in America to special dance faculties, and establishment in the Soviet Union of institutes for the study of choreography. And dance notation promised great advances in recording specific choreographies and as a basic linguistic tool in dance education.

# TWYLA THARP

Born on July 1, 1941, in Portland, Indiana, Twyla Tharp is a popular American dancer, director, and choreographer noted for her innovation and for the humour she brought to much of her work.

Tharp grew up in her native Portland and in Los Angeles; her childhood included comprehensive training in music and dance. While a student at Barnard College in New York City, she studied at the American Ballet Theatre School and received instruction from Richard Thomas, Martha Graham, and Merce Cunningham, among others. In 1963, shortly before her graduation from Barnard, she joined the Paul Taylor Dance Company, where she soon established herself as a dancer of considerable talent and imagination. In 1965 she formed her own troupe.

Tharp's first publicly performed piece of choreography, *Tank Dive*, was presented in 1965 at Hunter College. Over the next several years she choreographed numerous pieces, many of which employed street clothes, a bare stage, and no music. With her offbeat, technically precise explorations of various kinds and combinations of movements, she built a small but devoted following. In 1971

Tharp adopted jazz music and began creating dances that appealed to larger audiences. Her choreography retained its technical brilliance, often overlaid with an air of nonchalance, while its touches of flippant humour became more marked. Her pieces, most notably *The Fugue* (1970), *Deuce Coupe* (1973), *Push Comes to Shove* (1976), and *Baker's Dozen* (1979), established Tharp as one of the most innovative and popular modern choreographers. In addition, she created pieces for motion pictures such as *Hair* (1979), *Ragtime* (1981), and *Amadeus* (1984). In 1988 she disbanded her company and joined American Ballet Theatre, where she served as artistic associate until 1990. Tharp's autobiography, *Push Comes to Shove*, was published in 1992. She also wrote *The Creative Habit: Learn It and Use It for Life* (2003) and, with Jesse Kornbluth, *The Collaborative Habit: Life Lessons for Working Together* (2009). In 2002, Tharp directed *Movin' Out*, a dance-musical show set to the music and lyrics of Billy Joel, which opened on Broadway in New York City. Tharp directed *The Times They Are A-Changin'*, another dance-musical, but set to the lyrics and music of Bob Dylan, which opened in

*(continued on the next page)*

*(continued from the previous page)*

2006 in San Diego, California. In 2008 she was the recipient of the Jerome Robbins Prize for excellence in dance, as well as a Kennedy Center honoree. *Sinatra: Dance With Me*, a Las Vegas show that Tharp directed, premiered in 2010. In 2015 Tharp and her 12-member dance ensemble launched a 50th anniversary tour across the United States, in honor of the 1965 debut of her first dance, *Tank Dive.*

# DANCE IN MUSICAL THEATRE

Americans also created the most vital forms of theatrical dancing. The first musical stage performance seen in the United States was a ballad opera called *Flora*, produced in Charleston, South Carolina, in 1735. More than a century later, *The Black Crook* (1866) also scored an enormous success. It was not until the 20th century, however, that dancing and drama became truly integrated. Credit for this breakthrough goes to Agnes de Mille, whose *Oklahoma!* (1943) made dancing an integral part of the story. Performed by dancers who had studied ballet, the dances in *Oklahoma!* included not just ballet steps but folk dance and modern dance as well.

In musicals of both stage and screen, dance is an essential ingredient along with song, acting, and spectacle. Although the dancing is often mechanical and unoriginal, in the work of such dancers and choreographers as Fred Astaire and Gene Kelly it can rise to the status of a genuine art form. Sometimes, as in Jerome Robbins's choreography for the dances of the rival gangs in *West Side Story* (1957), it creates a powerful dramatic effect and brings a new vitality to the musical theatre. Robbins, in his turn, influenced other choreographers such as Bob Fosse, particularly known for his work on the film *All That Jazz* (1979), and Michael Bennett.

# HIP-HOP AND BREAK DANCING

Hip-hop is the cultural movement that attained widespread popularity in the 1980s and '90s. Although widely considered a synonym for rap music, the term hip-hop refers to a complex culture comprising four elements: deejaying, or turntabling; rapping, also known as MCing or rhyming; graffiti painting, also known as graf or writing; and B-boying, which encompasses hip-hop dance, style, and attitude, along with the sort of virile body language that philosopher Cornel West described as "postural semantics." Hip-hop originated in the predominantly African American economically depressed South Bronx section of New York City in the late 1970s. As the hip-hop movement began at society's margins, its origins are shrouded in myth, enigma, and obfuscation.

Graffiti and break dancing, the aspects of the culture that first caught public attention, had the least lasting effect.

The beginnings of the dancing, rapping, and deejaying components of hip-hop were bound together by the shared environment in which these art forms evolved. The first major hip-hop deejay (disc jockey) was DJ Kool Herc (Clive Campbell), an 18-year-old immigrant who introduced the huge sound systems of his native Jamaica to inner-city parties. Using two turntables, he melded percussive fragments from older records with popular dance songs to create a continuous flow of music. Kool Herc and other pioneering hip-hop deejays such as Grand Wizard Theodore, Afrika Bambaataa, and Grandmaster Flash isolated and extended the break beat (the part of a dance record where all sounds but the drums drop out), stimulating improvisational dancing. Contests developed in which the best dancers created break dancing, a style with a repertoire of acrobatic and occasionally airborne moves, including gravity-defying head spins and backspins. In 2015 the Museum of the City of New York presented the works of some photographers who documented the hip-hop era in an exhibition entitled *Hip-Hop Revolution: Photographs* by Janette Beckman, Joe Conzo, and Martha Cooper. The exhibition brought together the influences of music, dance, and fashion on hip-hop culture.

Break dancing is an energetic form of dance, popularized by African Americans and U.S. Latinos, that includes stylized footwork and athletic moves such as spinning on the knees, hands, or head. Break dancing originated in New York City during the late 1960s and early 1970s from martial arts moves developed by street gangs. The moves, originally learned as a form of self-defense against other gangs, eventually evolved into the complex and athletic moves that characterize modern break dancing.

Break dancing is largely improvisational, without "standard" moves or steps. The emphasis is on energy, movement, creativity, and an element of danger. It is meant to convey the rough world of the street gangs from which it sprang. It is also associated with a particular style of dressing that includes baggy pants or sweat suits, baseball caps worn sideways or backward, and sneakers (required because of the dangerous nature of many of the moves).

The term *break* refers to the particular rhythms and sounds produced by deejays by mixing sounds from records to produce a continuous dancing beat. The technique was pioneered by Kool DJ Herc, who mixed the percussion "breaks" from two identical records. By playing the breaks repeatedly and switching from one record to the other, Kool Herc cre-

A team of dancers from Poland perform during a hip-hop, break dance, and electric boogie (also called electric slide) world dance championship in Germany. Hip-hop and break dancing have had an extraordinary influence on the modern dance styles of many countries.

ated what he called cutting breaks. During his live performances at New York dance clubs, Kool Herc would shout, "B-Boys go down!"—the signal for dancers to perform the gymnastic moves that are the hallmark of break dancing.

From these early roots, break-dancers began to add different moves to their routines, such as "pops" and "locks," which brought a robotic quality to the dance. This style was popularized in the early 1970s by artists, including Charlie Robot, who appeared on the popular *Soul Train* television program. Disco dancers began to emulate these moves, which then entered the mainstream disco culture. However, at this time, break dancing and the hip-hop culture from which it emerged were still associated with crime and gang violence.

In the 1980s break dancing reached a greater audience when it was adopted by mainstream artists such as Michael Jackson. Jackson's "moonwalk," a step that involved sliding backward and lifting the soles of the feet so that he appeared to be gliding or floating, became a sensation among teens of all races. Record producers, seeing the growing popularity of the genre, signed artists who could imitate the street style of the break-dancers while presenting a more wholesome image that would appeal to mainstream audiences. Break dancing had gone from a street phenomenon to one that was embraced by the wider culture. The dance style appeared in several movies including *Wild Style* (1982), *Breakin'* (1984), and *Beat Street* (1984).

Break dancing had an enormous influence on modern dance styles, and offshoots of it were performed in many music and especially rap videos as well as in live concerts by popular artists such as Britney Spears. The mainstreaming of the genre was never more clearly demonstrated than in 2004, when break-dancers were invited to perform in the Vatican in Rome before Pope John Paul II.

# CHAPTER FOUR

# FOLK DANCE

**W**hen tribal societies in Europe gave way to more structured societies, the old dance forms gradually developed into what are now called folk or peasant dances. For a long time these retained much of their original significance and therefore could have received the modern classification of "ethnic." The Maypole dance, still sometimes performed in England, is a descendant of older tree-worshipping dances, the ribbons that the dancers hold as they dance around the pole symbolize the tree's branches. The Morris dance, also called the moresque because the blackened faces of the dancers resembled the Moors, is a survival of early weapon dances, which were not war dances but an ancient form of religious worship. The types and styles of these different dances were numerous, and, as with tribal dances, many were lost so that information about them often remains sketchy. In the 20th century, efforts to collect national music and dances were made by, among others, Cecil Sharp in England and Béla Bartók in Hungary. These efforts resulted in the revival of certain dances, but they are now danced mainly for recreation, and their original significance has been lost. It is in this conscious revival or preservation of ethnic and national dances for purposes of entertainment that modern folk dance has its origin.

Although different areas and countries have different styles of dance, most of them share common formations and styles of movement. The earliest and simplest formation, the closed circle, is found in all folk dances and derives from the ritual of circling around an object of worship. The dancers grasp one another by the hands, wrists, shoulders, elbows, or waists and face the centre of the circle. In more complex forms, dancers move into and out of the circle to perform individual movements or to join into

These men are performing the traditional Bulgarian *horo* dance in the icy winter water of the Tundzha River in Kalofer, Bulgaria. The *horo* is a communal folk dance of Bulgaria and is danced in linked circles, in serpentine chains, and in straight lines.

couples, or, as the dancers circle, they may weave around one another. In some dances there are two concentric circles, sometimes the inner one of men and the outer one of women.

Another common formation, the chain, involves a long line of dancers, often holding hands or linked by handkerchiefs. The leader may trace a complex, serpentine pattern for the others to follow. Processional dances may travel a long way—even through an entire village. The dancers are mostly in couples, with the procession halting at times for them to dance together.

Many folk dances today are performed in sets, groups of about eight dancers who may perform in all of the above formations but within a restricted space. In other dances, individuals may leave the group and dance on their own.

Folk dance steps are usually quite simple variations on walking, hopping, skipping, and turning. Depending on the particular dance form, these steps may be long, slow, and gliding or short, fast, and springing. The hips are usually held still, though in more vigorous dances the men in particular may crouch, kneel, or even lie on the floor. Some dances involve large jumps and lifts, usually with the man seizing the woman by the waist, lifting her into the air, and possibly turning with her.

There are numerous kinds of holds. For example, two dancers may face each other and hold hands with the arms crossed, link arms, or use a hold similar to that of ballroom dancers.

Individual folk dances may also contain distinctive motifs: the dancers may clap their hands, wave handkerchiefs, or clash sticks with one another. Some dances contain elements of mime—not only the bows and curtsies of courtship dance but also gestures such as those performed in certain Slavic harvest dances, where the arms are brought up to the chest and opened outward as if presenting something.

Many European folk dances are characterized by a strong emphasis on pattern and formation. The dancers frequently move in an ordered relation to one another, and the steps follow clearly delineated floor patterns on the ground. The circle is the simplest pattern, but the chain, the procession, and the "longways" dance (in which facing rows of couples walk or skip briskly through maneuvers instructed by a caller) are also common. Although there are numerous exceptions to the rule, the emphasis in many of those dances is on the footwork, rather than on large or vigorous movements of the body.

## COLLECTOR JOHN PLAYFORD AND THE PRESERVATION OF DANCE

As early as the 17th century, dances performed by rural folk ("country dances") were collected and distributed through popular publications for public distribution. Typically, country dances are characterized by "long-ways" formations. The 17th-century English music publisher and bookseller John Playford edited and published as many as 900 country dances through seven editions of *The English Dancing Master*. The first was published in 1651. His work was carried on after his death by his son Henry through the 17th and final edition in 1728; after the first edition the work bore the abridged title *The Dancing Master*.

The Playford dances are still consulted, especially in the United Kingdom and the United States. Those dances, which were transmitted from person to person before being published, have been preserved in the same form through many generations. The publication allowed a different sort of dancer—a city office worker, perhaps—to perform country dances of another time and place. Questions of whether such dances are folk dances and whether modern groups performing them are folk dancers remain a matter of controversy. But most contemporary groups who dance the country dances consider themselves to be folk dancers and the dances to be folk dances.

The late 18th and 19th centuries were an especially vibrant period in Europe and the Americas. It was a time of intellectual and artistic efflorescence: the Enlightenment, the Industrial Revolution, Nationalism, and Romanticism. People increasingly depended upon the written word to record and convey ideas. Literacy defined a class of people, often even more than family pedigree. Literate persons usually lived in urban areas, a demographic fact that led to the perception of rural people as belonging to a lower class than those from urban areas. At the same time, the complications of urban life made the perceived simplicity of the country attractive.

## COLLECTOR JOHANN GOTTFRIED VON HERDER AND THE IDEA OF THE FOLK

The late 18th-century German critic, theologian, and philosopher Johann Gottfried von Herder was apparently the first to use the word *folk* (in German, as *Volk*) in print. Herder recorded and analyzed Germanic languages at a time when Germany was beginning to emerge as an identifiable political entity from a collection of principalities and city-states. Herder, who was particularly interested in traditional song texts, published collections of old songs from many parts of the world. In his research he discovered many traditional Germanic songs, tales, and customs transmitted by ordinary people who lived customary lifestyles. They were Herder's *Volk*. Herder collected folk traditions, including folk dances, to prevent their loss and to encourage nationalistic pride.

Into the 19th century, throughout Europe, more and more agrarian workers emigrated from the farms and small towns to find employment in the new factories of the cities. Those people who still pursued an agrarian lifestyle, often bereft of formal education, were dismissed by the literate as backward, even inferior "folk." Yet as they seemed in danger of extinction, they became viewed with nostalgia, especially by Romantics in Germany and elsewhere. Their way of life seemed simpler and unspoiled. Collecting the remembered traditions of the folk became a popular and respected activity.

One consequence was the forming of an image of the happy peasant. Painters, writers, musicians, and choreographers portrayed this character in their arts. Musicians wrote "dances" that were not danced. Dance academies often adopted particular movements and whole dances from the idealized folk.

# WILLIAM JOHN THOMS AND FOLKLORISTICS

The English antiquarian William John Thoms (using the pseudonym Ambrose Merton) coined the English word *folklore* in August 1846, taking credit in a letter to the periodical *The Athenaeum.*

Four years later, his pride as inventor of the term was restated in *Notes and Queries,* a weekly publication that he founded in 1849 and edited for 23 years and that continued to be published into the 21st century. Both publications began to accept submissions relating to the preservation of folklore. It is clear from discussions in his periodical that Thoms did not mean anything more specific by folk than "people of older times."

Two dance games are mentioned repeatedly by the magazine's correspondents in the 1850–52 period, and they are never associated with class, occupation, education, or residence: "London Bridge Is Broken Down," for children, and the "Cushion Dance," for adults. The first may be related to London Bridge, a round-dance game that in its various forms (including "London Bridge Is Falling Down") continued to be played by children in the early 21st century. The second is a round-dance kissing game in which a solo dancer carries a cushion into the center of a circle of other dancers while they all sing a song. At the end of the song, the solo dancer drops the cushion in front of someone of the opposite sex; the chosen person kneels on the cushion and is kissed by the soloist. The kissed person becomes the soloist, and the previous soloist joins the circle. The action repeats until everyone has been kissed and has danced in the centre. The cushion dance was done at weddings and seems to have been popular in England and Germany.

The correspondents to *Notes and Queries*, in what was a 19th-century equivalent of a chat room, sought to establish the games' texts and origins. Since the magazine's beginning, "old-time" dances have been discussed often—dancing games, contra dances, quadrilles, jigs, reels, and so forth. The occasions for dancing, such as Christmas, weddings, and balls, are also mentioned, but the performers are not. The magazine has played an important part in preserving accounts of old dances.

The study of folklore and its variants quickly took hold in scholarly circles in Great Britain and the United States. The term *folklore* soon acquired a formal discipline of theories and methods for research as well as a forum for the exchange of information and ideas. The discipline was called folkloristics. By 1878 the Folklore Society had been founded in England. In 1888 the American Folklore Society was founded and began to publish the *Journal of American Folklore.* By 1890 the Folklore Society in England had begun publishing its peer-reviewed journal, *Folk-lore.* Both societies and their journals were still operating in the 21st century.

By the end of the 19th century, many collectors around the world had been working to document and archive their national folk arts. The 19th-century Polish collector Oskar Kolberg, for example, had published nearly 70 volumes documenting Polish folk dancing; he is but one of dozens of scholars, antiquarians, and visionaries who have a place in the annals of early folk dance scholarship. Following the collectors were revival movements, folk dance societies, museums, and archives.

## CECIL SHARP AND THE PROMOTION OF FOLK DANCE

The English musician Cecil Sharp was a teacher and principal of London's Hampstead Conservatory of Music. According to his colleague and biographer Maud Karpeles, Sharp saw his first English Morris dances in 1899. He was inspired by this experience, having thought previously that English folk songs and dances were extinct.

For the remainder of his life, Sharp collected and promoted English traditional songs and folk dances. He began publishing those songs in 1907, followed by works on Morris dances (five volumes, 1909–13), sword dances of Northern England (three volumes, 1912–13), and country dances (six volumes, 1909–27; the last volumes were posthumous). In 1911 he founded the English Folk Dance Society—complete with a prescribed repertoire, grade levels, and examinations—to train folk dance

England's Glory Ladies Morris dancers perform in Bledington, Oxfordshire. This particular group performs dances such as hanky dances, stick dances, garland dances, clapping dances, Morris jigs, and reels at folk festivals and other events.

teachers and demonstrate folk dance performances. The evidence suggests that Sharp believed that the forms he tried to maintain were revivals of ancient dances, originally developed by rural folk from ritual origins.

From 1914 to 1919 Sharp and Karpeles visited the United States. In Appalachian Mountain communities they found many old dances and songs taken to the Americas by settlers of Scottish and Irish ancestry. Some of these were still being performed in England, but others were preserved only in the United States. The most celebrated of these dances Sharp named the Kentucky running set; it was a longways dance of the country-dance style, in which two lines of dancers facing one another "reel off" so that each couple in turn moves to the beginning of the paired line. In 1915 Sharp encouraged the development of an American branch of the English Folk Dance Society. The Country Dance and Song Society was thus established; it was still active in the early 21st century.

# BÉLA BARTÓK AND ETHNOGRAPHIC SCHOLARSHIP

The Hungarian composer Béla Bartók was inspired by the folk music and dances that he collected and analyzed and used as themes in his compositions. As an avid field worker he experienced firsthand the music and dance of Hungary, Slovakia, Romania, Bulgaria, Moldavia, and Yugoslavia, as well as Turkey, Algeria, and Morocco. He was probably the first musicologist to bridge East and West. Although he worked with folk materials throughout his career, from 1912 through 1915 he devoted himself almost entirely to the collection and study of folk music and dances. In the field he enjoyed and

These folk dancers perform a dance in Budapest, Hungary. The Hungarian composer Béla Bartók incorporated a number of settings of folk songs for his musical pieces for voice and piano. He also devoted himself to composing and studying collections of folk music.

participated in the folk culture of his hosts. As a musicologist he recorded with the equipment available at that time, took extensive notes, and analyzed his material in detail. World War I ended his extended collecting expeditions; in 1940 he moved to New York, where he again focused on his ethnomusicological work. Bartók is but one of a long list of distinguished scholars who have researched Hungarian folk dances. But Bartók ranged farther in his explorations of other eastern European regions, as well as of Arabic and Turkish cultures.

## LJUBICA JANKOVIĆ AND DANICA JANKOVIĆ AND MODERN SCHOLARSHIP

Two sisters from Serbia, Ljubica Janković (1894–1974) and Danica Janković (1898–

1960), devoted much of their lives to collecting and analyzing folk dances from southeastern Europe. Between 1934 and 1964 they published eight volumes and several monographs of dance research. In the work they analyzed about 900 dances, describing choreography, music, and costume. They wrote about the cultural background and preservation of the dances, and, especially noteworthy, they recognized the contribution of "gifted dancers" to the refinement of the dances. The adaptation of a dance for the stage, they felt, took that dance out of the folk realm and made it an adapted dance; they refused to call anything a folk dance except an anonymously created dance performed in traditional settings. The Janković sisters coined the term *paraphrased folk dance* for adapted dances.

Other scholars continued to struggle with terminology and the differences between dances in traditional cultures and their derivatives in other contexts. In his influential article for the *Journal of the International Folk Music Council* titled "Once Again: On the Concept of 'Folk Dance'" (1968), the German folklorist Felix Hoerburger observed that folk dances generally fell into two categories: first, dances that were transmitted through the generations by members of a traditional culture, and second, dances that were derived from the first category but performed by different dancers for different reasons. He labeled these "first existence" and "second existence," respectively. Although the labels were useful, they presented their own problems. But scholars have yet to agree on a unified approach to researching and analyzing folk dances.

In the early 20th century, social and educational reformers, many of them influenced by the educator John Dewey, foresaw many benefits to the wide teaching of folk dances. At the University of Chicago, Dewey established and directed the experimental Laboratory Schools, which opened in 1896. He championed the use of folk dancing in the classroom as a means of physical education and as an example of what he called art as experience transposed into creative imagination. Several of his students went on to develop his ideas; two of the most successful were Elizabeth Burchenal and Mary Wood Hinman.

## AMERICAN TEACHER ELIZABETH BURCHENAL

In 1903 the American educator Elizabeth Burchenal introduced folk dancing as physical education at Teachers College of Columbia University in New York. Later, as athletics inspector for the New York City public schools, she introduced folk dancing into the curriculum. She organized annual folk dance festivals for schoolgirls; by 1913, 10,000 girls were doing Maypole dances in the New York City borough parks. For six years she travelled and studied folk dances in several European countries and published many books about the folk dances she learned. She and her sister Ruth established the Folk Arts Center in New York City, with exhibition galleries and an archive of American folk dance. Elizabeth Burchenal was also one of the founders of the American Folk Dance Society.

## AMERICAN EDUCATOR MARY WOOD HINMAN

Another American scholar and teacher, Mary Wood Hinman, worked in New York and Chicago to train teachers and encourage folk dancing among local ethnic organizations. After traveling to several countries to learn folk dances, she developed a teacher-training school in Chicago that prepared women to teach folk dances in schools, parks, and settlement houses. (Teaching at a Chicago private school as well, she inspired and encouraged the future great modern dancer Doris Humphrey.) In 1930 she helped establish the Folk Festival Council of New York; this private service organization sponsored folk dance festivals with performers from numerous ethnic organizations. In addition, she developed and taught a course titled Dances of Many Peoples at what is now the New School in Manhattan.

# THE SETTLEMENT MOVEMENT

Both Burchenal and Hinman participated in the settlement movement, an idealistic social-welfare movement begun in the late 19th century. In the larger U.S. cities of the early 20th century, neighbourhood institutions called settlement houses fostered the health of urban neighbourhoods and their inhabitants through education, recreation, and social services. Folk dancing served several of the organizations' goals, furthering individual health through exercise and recreation as well as neighbourhood vitality through mutual acceptance and appreciation. Immigrant women could perform dances of their youth to remain connected with their past and feel accepted in their new country, and people could learn dances from many nations, ideally learning an appreciation of their neighbours' heritages. These organizations were especially active in Chicago and New York.

Some of the folk dance teachers who worked in the settlement houses made lasting contributions. Michael Herman and Mary Ann Herman, for example, developed a series of sound recordings of the music for folk dances from many parts of the world. With the recordings, dances could be performed even when live musicians were unavailable. Yet the use of recordings had a lasting effect on the form of the folk dances that were being taught outside of their original setting. Early recordings were no more than three minutes in length, so a new time restriction went into effect. And the unchanging music meant codified, unchanging dances.

# THE INTERNATIONAL FOLK DANCE MOVEMENT

Another outstanding and influential teacher from the settlement movement was Vytautas Finadar (Vyts) Beliajus, a Lithuanian who immigrated to the United States as a teenager. His family joined relatives in the Lithuanian community in Chicago. He organized the Lithuanian Youth Society, where he taught folk dancing; the group performed at the 1933 Chicago World's Fair. He soon expanded his expertise to include Mexican, Hindi, Italian, and Hasidic Jewish dances. In 1942 he started a newsletter for dancers who were overseas in the armed forces during World War II. The newsletter developed into the journal *Viltis* (Lithuanian for "hope"), which covered all aspects of folk dance for the hobbyist. He continued to edit the journal until his death in 1994. Although he was not a scholar or traveling collector, he was a major influence on the international folk dance movement in the United States.

The broader folk dance movement gained momentum in California, inspired by a Chinese American man, Song Chang, and his Swedish wife, Harriet, who wanted to re-create the camaraderie they experienced while folk dancing during a visit to Europe. They and their friends organized a group called Chang's International Folk Dancers. The group performed at San Francisco's Golden Gate Exhibition (1939–40).

In the 21st century the international folk dance movement remained one of the most active repositories of folk dances and their performance. Its members learned dances from all over the world, without regard to their own ethnic background. They borrowed or adapted folk dances that were culturally foreign to them, and they did not consider themselves to be the "folk." The dances in their repertory were generally handed down by someone else's ancestors and not their own.

The dances of the international folk dance movement became increasingly pop- ular with recreational dancers, at first in the United States and eventually in countries around the world. The dances—most of them from Europe, with a few from North America and Japan—were codified and decontextualized so that dancers could perform them any place in the world.

# FOLK DANCE IN THE UNITED STATES

The folk dance movement spread in unexpected ways. In the United States the industrialist Henry Ford promoted the square dance by organizing square-dancing parties for thousands of people, especially his employees and their families. In 1926 he built Lovett Hall, an enormous dance hall in Dearborn, Michigan, to encourage square dancing, partly to counteract what was commonly seen as the lascivious nature of popular dances such as the Charleston. Until 2005 square dancers continued to meet at Lovett Hall.

Square dancing has an honoured place as an American folk dance, although Congress has never declared a national dance. Other forms of dancing have also been identified as American folk dances, such as Appalachian clogging, Cajun dancing, country (including contra) dancing, and line dancing. Included in the folk dance category by some commentators are Native American powwow dancing, African American dances first known among slaves in the Sea Islands of Georgia (such as "patting Juba" and the "ring shout"), the step dancing that was developed by young African

American men, the dances done by Mardi Gras groups from Louisiana, and the domesticated dances of various immigrant groups.

Throughout North America groups keep their cultural ties and heritage alive by sharing their folk dances with their children and with each other. These domestic groups are not part of the international folk dance movement, nor are they folkloric troupes performing for tourist events. Rather, they represent a joyful way to preserve an ethnic legacy. In Hawaii, for example, folk dance groups represent Asian countries, Pacific Island countries, Puerto Rico, Portugal, and Scotland, among other places. California's ethnic dance groups include representation from the Balkan countries, Iran, India, and Latin America; an annual ethnic dance festival in San Francisco showcases their work. The annual Holiday Folk Fair in Milwaukee, Wisconsin, has drawn thousands of amateur dancers since 1944. New York City's immigrant groups from hundreds of countries celebrate cultural events with folk dancing. South Florida is especially rich in groups that celebrate their Caribbean heritage with dance. In Phoenix, immigrants of East African and Southeast Asian origin meet in dance halls, bars, or homes to do folk dances to popular music. Folk dancing persists anywhere immigrants have settled, and the dancing public is larger and more diverse than it may at first appear.

# THE USE OF FOLK DANCE TO SUPPORT NATIONALISM

Folk dances and their association with national identity have made them vehicles for government propaganda. In Nazi Germany in the 1930s and 1940s, the government used charming folk dances to embody the mystique of an idyllic Germany. These folk dances were expected to engender loyalty and the kind of national pride that served the ideology of the Third Reich; Germans were to be knit into a unified and supposedly superior "race," in part through such activities.

Folk dances were pulled from their normal contexts to become national symbols to the outside world in the years after World War II, especially in communist countries. Gifted dancers were selected and professionally trained to perform theatrically enhanced and decontextualized folk dances. The resulting "folk dance" troupes would tour the world as evidence of the success of their governments in unifying their countries and earning the support of the "folk." Most of these companies represented eastern European nations, including Romania, Bulgaria, the former Czechoslovakia (now the Czech Republic and Slovakia), and the former

Yugoslavia (now Serbia, Montenegro, Bosnia and Herzegovina, Croatia, Macedonia, Slovenia, and Kosovo). Similarly, certain governments—for example, those of North Korea and China—have used dance in mass performances to symbolize the people's support of their political systems.

## FOSTERING GOODWILL AND MAKING A PROFIT WITH FOLK DANCE

Not all ethnic and national performances are ideological in nature. The United Nations has encouraged cultural exchange as a means of fostering goodwill between countries. Cultural touring includes folk troupes, among others; to represent folk dance, the United States has supported a group from Berea, Kentucky, for example.

National, state, and local tourist agencies have gone beyond ambassadorship and have discovered the value of dances and dance troupes that are identified as their own. Visitors can be entertained, absorb some local culture, and support the economy. Around the world, from Mongolia to the remotest islands, dances are polished, choreographed, packaged, and presented as authentic.

Near the Olympic Velodrome at the Olympic Complex in Athens, Greece, a Greek folk dance group entertains the crowd in 2005. Folk dancing has been a way to enrich cultural exchanges of cooperation among nations.

## WHO OWNS THE DANCE?

In the 21st century, questions of ownership have reached far into the practice of music and dance. Several Native American groups and the Republic of Croatia, for example, have insisted that traditional arts should have the protection of copyright, so that they could gain recognition and control how performances would be used.

# DANCING FOR ENLIGHTENMENT

Two late 20th-century phenomena use folk dances as a medium to achieve idealistic ends. The two are Circle Dances and Dances of Universal Peace. The organizations have similar goals, but their histories differ and they are not connected.

The Circle Dance phenomenon was developed by the German dancer Bernard Wosien, who encountered circle-type folk dances in his European travels and was impressed with the spirituality they inspired in him. He found an established spiritual and ecological community at Findhorn, Scotland, and joined the group in 1976. More dance groups formed in Scotland and England and spread from there. The repertory grew with the number of teachers. The dances became known by several names, including world dances, circle dances, or the original sacred circle dances. Circles are unbroken, and dancers move as one; these characteristics became part of a view of the act of doing the dances as a meditative or spiritual experience. The phenomenon has spread in person and on the Internet; the dances are relatively simple to learn and teach. Laura Shannon, a dancer, teacher, and writer

*(continued on the next page)*

*(continued from the previous page)*

who lived in Findhorn, was instrumental in spreading the movement; she was especially interested in the dances of Armenia, Greece, and the Balkans.

The Dances of Universal Peace were developed by Samuel Lewis from California, who was a Sufi and Zen master. He had been a student of modern dance pioneer Ruth St. Denis, who inspired him with her understanding of dance as a means to attain wisdom. In the late 1960s, he and some followers began performing folk dances as a spiritual practice, and soon the movement gained momentum. Lewis died in 1971, but his foundation continued to draw on many of the world's mystical and religious traditions. The more than 500 dances in the repertory are accompanied by lyrics representing the various sacred foundations of the dances. Members carry their dances to many countries in their quest to encourage peace and intercultural harmony.

Performing groups and organizations in Great Britain resisted laws that would require the licensing of all music, live or recorded, used for dance. Similarly, the U.S. Congress was considering questions of the ownership and copyright of intangible assets in the United States. In folk music and folk dance, which were long considered to be anonymously created and commonly owned—that is, in the public domain—challenges to the status quo became more common. Groups were claiming to be the "folk" and asserting rights. Once again, questions of authenticity and provenance arose, and dancers and scholars had to reexamine their definitions of folk dance and folk dancers. The United Nations has been working on the matter from several directions: In 2003 the United Nations Educational, Scientific and Cultural Organization (UNESCO) adopted the Convention for the Safeguarding of the Intangible Cultural Heritage to establish an approach to the preservation and protection of nonmaterial cultural properties such as dance, language, ritual, and craftsmanship, and in the first decade of the 21st century the World Intellectual Property Organization of the UN was actively working to establish how property rights extended to traditional knowledge.

# CONCLUSION

Although the exact origins of dance are unknown, cave paintings left by prehistoric peoples seem to indicate that even the earliest peoples danced. Dance may have been used to express emotion or to communicate with others before there was language. The early cave paintings suggest that prehistoric peoples also danced to control the events of their lives.

For the ancient Egyptians, dance was a crucial element in the festivals held for Isis and Osiris, who were among the most important gods of ancient Egypt. For the ancient Greeks dance was an important feature of religious rites, or ceremonies, as well as everyday life. The dances associated with the god Dionysus were so elaborate that they led to the development of Greek drama in the 5th century BCE. Festivals in ancient Rome honouring Roman gods featured dances, and wealthy young Romans attended dancing classes. Dances were also part of the drama. By about the 1st century CE, however, the Romans preferred spectacular shows featuring many different elements.

Toward the end of the Roman era, Christianity began to take hold in Europe and ushered in the period called the Middle Ages. Once again dance was used in religious ceremonies along with music and dramatic dialogue. Some dances celebrated religious feast days, but others celebrated the changing of the seasons and good harvests.

At the same time, new kingdoms were being formed throughout Europe. Dance became an important part of the life of the royal courts of these kingdoms. The members of the court learned to dance and to move gracefully. Ordinary people had their own dances, too. The peasants' dances eventually became the ethnic and folk dances of today, while the court dances evolved into social dance.

In about the late 1300s, the Renaissance began in Europe. It was a time of great learning and attention to the arts, including dance. During this period dance came to be seen as not simply a form of entertainment but also a form of art. As in the days of ancient Greece, dance became associated with the theatre. People known as dancing masters were hired to teach members of the court. They also began to transform dances into short dramas by framing them with a theme or subject. The courts began to put on festive pageants in which the dancers wore costumes and combined dance with music. At first these were performed only by members of the court, but professional dancers began to emerge at the end of the 5th century BCE.

Meanwhile the court pageants became more and more elaborate. A work created in 1581 for the queen of France, *Ballet comique de la reine* ("comic ballet of the queen"), is said to be the first true ballet. The work launched the form known as *ballet de cour* (court ballet), in which the French monarchs themselves participated. When the French king Louis XIV decided to stop participating in theatrical presentations in the late 1600s so did the other nobility. The dances then moved to theatres with professional dancers. This marked the beginning of ballet as a form of theatrical dancing separate from the social dancing that court members continued to perform at court for their own amusement.

Ballet became extremely popular in 18th-century France. Individual performers often added steps and gestures of their own, and it was during this time that the first great soloists were recognized. In the 19th century a French choreographer named Marius Petipa went to Russia and helped make that country the centre of the dance world. The Russian promoter and manager Serge Diaghilev spread the Russian ballet (the Ballets Russes) through Europe and the Americas in the early 20th century.

In the 18th century social dancing moved outside the courts to ballrooms and private houses, where more people were able to participate. Over the years various dance forms went in and out of style. Some of the most popular were the minuet in the 17th and 18th centuries and the waltz in the 18th and 19th. Many popular social dances were adapted from folk dances, such as the polka and the mazurka. Today most folk dances live through ballet. The leaps of the male dancer that win great applause—the entrechat and the cabriole—developed from the jumps of the peasants. The classical pas de deux, in which a couple dances alternately together and separately, is a highly refined courtship dance. Many individual ballets have folk dance themes. The ballet sequences of the musical *Oklahoma!* are elaborations of American folk dances.

A new tradition in theatrical dance was born at the beginning of the 20th century when the American dancer Isadora Duncan started what is known as modern dance. Rather than changing the standard postures and steps in ballet, Duncan did not use them at all. Her new form of dance was free spirited and highly personal. Several dancers carried on the style of Duncan, but none was as influential as the American Martha Graham. Her company and her school trained generations of devoted students.

The American choreographer Agnes de Mille made dancing an important part of musical theatre in 1943. Her production of the musical *Oklahoma!* in that year featured a combination of ballet, folk dance, and modern dance. The dances choreographed by Jerome Robbins for *West Side Story* (1957) brought a new urban aesthetic to musical theatre.

Europeans brought their dances with them when they settled in the Americas. By the

In 1947 the saloon girls dance the cancan during the extended dream ballet sequence in the production of *Oklahoma!* Choreographer Agnes de Mille, who won many prizes and awards for her ballets, further developed the narrative aspect of dance and made innovative use of American themes, folk dances, and physical idioms in her choreography.

20th century, however, many dances had originated from within the Americas and then migrated to Europe. These include the tango from Latin America and dances associated with the jazz movement in the United States, such as the Charleston. As music became less formal so did dances. Popular music, from big band to rock and roll to hip-hop, continues to inspire new forms of social dancing.

*The History of Western Dance* has examined for readers the various influences on and developments in Western dance performance from ancient times to the present, noting where appropriate the impact of other cultures.

# GLOSSARY

**acolyte**  One that attends or assists; a follower.

**adagio**  In dance, a ballet duet by a man and woman or a trio of dancers displaying difficult feats of balance, lifting, or spinning.

**ascetic**  Practicing strict self-denial especially for religious discipline.

***branle***  A 12th-century French chain dance adopted during the Renaissance by European aristocrats, where the word "branle" was Anglicized as "brawl." It was named for its characteristic side-to-side movement and performed by a chain of dancers who alternated large sideways steps to the left with an equal number of smaller steps to the right.

**cabriole**  A ballet jump in which the dancer beats the calves of the legs together in the air, with a scissors-like movement. When the beat occurs, the legs are extended at either a 45° or 90° angle to the body at the front, side, or back.

**chaconne**  Originally a fiery and suggestive dance that appeared in Spain about 1600 and eventually gave its name to a musical form.

**choreographer**  A person who composes or arranges dances.

**corps de ballet**  A chorus of a ballet company.

**cracovienne** A Polish folk dance.

**Diaspora** The settling of scattered colonies of Jews outside Palestine after the Babylonian exile.

**ecstatic dance** A form of mass dance in which the experience of an inner vision of a god or of one's relation to or union with the divine is exemplified. In ancient Greece, the ecstatic dance was associated with the cult of Dionysus; in the Middle Ages a mass dance was usually performed in churchyards.

**entrechat** A jump in ballet, beginning in the fifth position, during which the dancer repeatedly crosses his straight legs at the lower calf.

**Expressionism** An artistic style in which the artist seeks to depict not objective reality but rather the subjective emotions and responses that objects and events arouse within a person. The Expressionist school in modern dance included Isadora Duncan, Martha Graham, Doris Humphrey, and Mary Wigman, among others.

**fandango** A lively Spanish or Spanish-American dance.

**flamenco** A vigorous rhythmic dance style of the Andalusian Gypsies.

**galliard** A lively dance with five steps to a phrase popular in the 16th century as a sequel to the stately pavane.

**galop** A lively dance in duple measure performed with sliding steps from side to side and popular in the 19th century.

**harlequinade** A play or pantomime in which the harlequin has a leading role.

**joculator** A wandering entertainer of medieval Europe who for hire practiced the arts of minstrelsy, narration, dancing, juggling, and mime.

**jota** A Spanish folk dance in ¾ time performed by a man and a woman to intricate castanet and heel rhythms.

**labyrinthine** Like a labyrinth, which is a structure of intricate passageways that make it difficult to find the way from the interior to the entrance or from the entrance to the center.

**lasciviousness** Lewdness or lust.

**lecherous** Arousing lust.

**longways** In two straight lines.

**maxixe** A ballroom dance of Brazilian origin roughly like the two-step.

**mazurka** A Polish dance in moderate triple measure often of varied steps and figures but having characteristically a slide and hop to the side.

**mime** The art of creating and portraying a character or narrating a story with body movement and facial expression.

**moresque** Having the characteristics of the Moors in Spain.

**Morris dance** A vigorous dance done by men wearing costumes and bells and carrying sticks or handkerchiefs and performed as a traditional part of English pageants, processions, and May Day games.

**pantomime** A performance in which a story is told without words by using body movements and facial expressions.

**pavane** A stately court dance by couples in ceremonial costume that was introduced from southern Europe into England in the 16th century.

**polonaise** A stately Polish processional dance fashionable in 19th-century Europe.

**sarabande** A stately court dance of the 17th and 18th centuries that resembles the minuet and that evolved from a quick Spanish dance.

**seguidilla** A Spanish dance having many regional variations in mood and tempo.

**spectacle** An eye-catching or dramatic public display.

**sylphid** A young imaginary or elemental being inhabiting the air and being mortal but soulless.

**troubadour** A strolling minstrel.

**volta** A 16th-century leaping and turning dance for couples.

**waltz** A ballroom dance in ¾ time with strong accent on the first beat.

# BIBLIOGRAPHY

## GENERAL WORKS ON DANCE

C. W. Beaumont, *Bibliography of Dancing* (1929). Anatole Chujoy and P. W. Manchester (comps. and eds.), *The Dance Encyclopedia*, rev. and enl. ed. (1967), a standard reference source with articles about all forms of dance, containing almost 300 photographs; G. B. L. Wilson, *A Dictionary of Ballet*, 3rd ed. (1974), a comprehensive reference source; and Curt Sachs, *World History of the Dance* (1937, reprinted 1965; originally published in German, 1933), a classic study of the dance in all forms, with special focus on origins, although some of Sachs's arguments have been challenged by more recent anthropological studies. Louis Horst, *Pre-Classic Dance Forms* (1937, reprinted 1968), a study of early dances; Richard Kraus and Sarah Alberti Chapman, *History of the Dance in Art and Education*, 2nd ed. (1981); and Walter Sorell, *Dance in Its Time* (1981), analyze the subject within a wide cultural and social context. Roger Copeland and Marshall Cohen (eds.), *What Is Dance?: Readings in Theory and Criticism* (1983), is a collection of essays on the nature of dance and its different styles and forms. Physiological aspects of dance and the mechanics of human movements are discussed in Kenneth Laws, *The Physics of Dance* (1984).

## THEATRICAL ASPECTS OF DANCING

Mary Clarke and Clement Crisp, *Making a Ballet* (1974), offers observations on the different relationships between choreographers and dancers, designers, and composers, and their *Design for Ballet* (1978) is a lavishly illustrated survey of costume and set design. Merle Armitage (ed.), *Martha Graham, the Early Years* (1937, reprinted 1978); and Le Roy Leatherman, *Martha Graham: Portrait of the Lady as an Artist* (1966), explore the nature of this prominent choreographer's work. See also David Vaughan, *Frederick Ashton and His Ballets* (1977); and Merce Cunningham, *Changes: Notes on Choreography,* edited by Frances Starr (1969). For the analysis of technical components of dance as theatre, see Elizabeth R. Hayes, *Dance Composition and Production for High Schools and Colleges* (1955, reissued 1981); Cyril W. Beaumont and Stanislas Idzikowski, *A Manual of the Theory and Practice of Classical Theatrical Dancing (Classical Ballet) (Cecchetti Method)*, rev. ed. (1977); and articles on the technical aspects of the art in *Dance Chronicle: Studies in Dance and the Related Arts* (quarterly).

# BALLET

Development of the ballet as a theatre art is reflected in the early writings of some dancing masters such as Cesare Negri Milanese, *Nuove inventioni di balli: opera vaghissima* (1604; reissued in 1969 as *Le gratie d'amore*), a richly illustrated treatise. See also Claude François Ménestrier, *Des Ballets anciens et modernes selon les régles du théâtre* (1682, reprinted 1972), the first printed history of the ballet; Deryck Lynham, *The Chevalier Noverre: Father of Modern Ballet* (1950, reprinted 1972), a biographical history; and Théophile Gautier, *The Romantic Ballet as Seen by Théophile Gautier*, trans. from French by Cyril W. Beaumont (1932, reprinted 1980). Lincoln Kirstein, *Dance: A Short History of Classic Theatrical Dancing* (1935, reprinted 1970), and *Movement & Metaphor* (1970, reissued as *Four Centuries of Ballet*, 1984), are brilliant analyses of the component parts of ballet and its developments, based on a wide survey of works. An authoritative historical study is Joan Lawson, *A History of Ballet and Its Makers* (1964, reprinted 1976). Selma Jeanne Cohen, *Next Week, Swan Lake: Reflections on Dance and Dances* (1982), is a witty and illuminating discussion of some basic issues in dance criticism. For the analysis of ballet techniques, see Jean-Georges Noverre, *Letters on Dancing and Ballets* (1930, reissued 1966; originally published in French, rev. ed. 1803–04), a reformer's statement of the principles of ballet techniques, which are still valid; and Carlo Blasis, *An Elementary Treatise upon the Theory and Practice of the Art of Dancing* (1944; originally published in French, 1820), a book by an Italian dancer and choreographer who codified the techniques of classic ballet. For the librettos of most famous ballets, see Cyril W. Beaumont, *Complete Book of Ballets: A Guide to the Principal Ballets of the Nineteenth and Twentieth Centuries*, rev. ed. (1949, reprinted 1956), supplemented with his *Ballets of Today* (1954), and *Ballets, Past & Present* (1955); and Walter Terry, *Ballet Guide: Background, Listings, Credits, and Descriptions of More Than Five Hundred of the World's Major Ballets* (1982). Contributions of the Russian ballet are discussed by Richard Buckle, *Diaghilev* (1979, reprinted 1984), and *Nijinsky*, 2nd ed. (1975); and by Natalia Roslavleva, *Era of the Russian Ballet* (1966, reprinted 1979). Lincoln Kirstein, *Thirty Years: The New York City Ballet* (Knopf, 1978). Bernard Taper, *Balanchine*, rev. ed. (1984).

# MODERN DANCE

Various aspects of modern dance and its forms are studied in Walter Terry, *The Dance in America*, rev. ed. (1971, reprinted 1981); Walter Sorell, *The Dance Has Many Faces*, 2nd ed. (1966); and John Martin, *Introduction to the Dance* (1939, reissued 1965), especially good on the theory of the early modern dance. Also see Selma Jeanne Cohen (ed.), *The Modern Dance: Seven Statements of Belief* (1966, reprinted 1973), a collection of essays by important choreographers; Sally Banes, *Terpsichore in Sneakers: Post-Modern Dance* (1980), a survey of the subject; and Joseph H. Mazo, *Prime Movers: The Makers of Modern Dance in America* (1977), which contains useful analyses of many choreographers' works. Current research in choreography is presented in the periodicals *Dancing Times* (monthly); *Dance Research Journal* (semiannual); and *Dance Magazine* (monthly). Agnes de Mille. *Dance to the Piper* (1980). Isadora Duncan, *My Life* (1972). Gelsey Kirkland and Greg Lawrence, *Dancing on My Grave* (1986). Keith Money, *Anna Pavlova* (1982). Ruth St. Denis, *An Unfinished Life* (1939).

# FOLK AND SOCIAL DANCE

Folk dance is the subject of Cecil J. Sharp and A. P. Oppé, *The Dance: An Historical Survey of Dancing in Europe* (1924, reprinted 1972); and Joan Lawson, *European Folk Dance* (1953, reprinted 1980). Periodicals include *Arabesque: A Magazine of International Dance* (bimonthly); *American Square Dance* (monthly); and *Square Dancing* (monthly). Social and ballroom dances are analyzed in Arthur H. Franks, *Social Dance: A Short History* (1963); and Philip J. S. Richardson, *The Social Dances of the Nineteenth Century in England* (1960).

The best reference works are two exhaustive sources of material. Bruno Nettl and Ruth M. Stone (eds.), *The Garland Encyclopedia of World Music*, 10 vol. (1998–2002), includes material on folk dances from all over the world; the set is a valuable resource for students of folk dance. Likewise, Selma Jeanne Cohen, *International Encyclopedia of Dance*, 6 vol. (1998), covers specific types of dance as well as the dance of many countries. Both of these sources are available online by subscription as well as in print.

Folk music, which is entwined with folk dance, is treated very well in Philip V. Bohlman,

*The Study of Folk Music in the Modern World* (1988). Other general treatments of value include Mary Clarke and Clement Crisp, *The History of Dance* (1981); Richard Crawford, *Introduction to America's Music* (2001); Marshall Stearns and Jean Stearns, *Jazz Dance: The Story of American Vernacular Dance*, updated ed. (1994), which shows how African American influences permeate popular dance forms in the world's cities; and Mary Bee Jensen and Clayne R. Jensen, *Folk Dancing*, new, enlarged ed. (1973).

Richard M. Dorson (ed.), *Folklore and Folklife: An Introduction* (1972), establishes the connection of all traditional performance, not just storytelling, to the field of folklore; another valuable general treatment is Robert A. Georges and Michael Owen Jones, *Folkloristics: An Introduction* (1995).

European dances have been exhaustively studied and presented by Nigel Allenby Jaffé and Margaret Allenby Jaffé in the European Folk Dance series, a collection of six works titled *10 Dances from...*, including Brittany, Denmark, Finland, Portugal, Sweden, and the Netherlands (1982–87); a summary treatment of the research is Margaret Allenby Jaffé, *National Dance* (2006). Specific regions are treated in György Martin, *Hungarian Folk Dances*, 2nd ed., rev., trans. from Hungarian (1988); and Mike Seeger and Ruth Pershing, *Talking Feet: Buck, Flatfoot, and Tap: Solo Southern Dance of the Appalachian, Piedmont, and Blue Ridge Mountain Regions* (1992). The influence of ritual is the subject of Iris J. Stewart, *Sacred Woman, Sacred Dance* (2000). Practical instruction is an important focus of Joan Lawson, *European Folk Dance: Its National and Musical Characteristics* (1953, reprinted 1980); and Beth Tolman and Ralph Page, *The Country Dance Book* (1937, reissued 1976).

Cecil J. Sharp contributed immeasurably to the field of dance research. A useful survey of his contribution is Maud Karpeles, *Cecil Sharp: His Life and Work* (1967). Among his own works are Cecil J. Sharp, *The Country Dance Book*, 6 vol. (1909–22, reissued from various editions, 6 vol. in 3, 1972–76), and *The Sword Dances of Northern England*, 3 vol., 2nd ed., rev. by Maud Karpeles (1951); Cecil J. Sharp and Herbert C. Macilwaine, *The Morris Book*, 5 vol., 2nd ed. (1911–24, reprinted 5 vol. in 2, 1974–75); and Cecil J. Sharp and A. P. Oppé, *The Dance: An Historical Survey of Dancing in Europe* (1924, reprinted 1972).

Two valuable essay collections are Ann Dils and Ann Cooper Albright (eds.), *Moving*

*History/Dancing Cultures: A Dance History Reader* (2001); and Maureen Needham (ed.), *I See America Dancing: Selected Readings, 1685–2000* (2002).

Political considerations in the promotion of folk dance are treated in Anthony Shay, "Parallel Traditions: State Folk Dance Ensembles and Folk Dance in 'The Field,'" *Dance Research Journal*, 31(1):29–56 (Spring 1999), which compares dances in different contexts; James R. Dow and Hannjost Lixfeld (eds. and trans.), *The Nazification of an Academic Discipline: Folklore in the Third Reich* (1994); and Naima Prevots, *Dance for Export: Cultural Diplomacy and the Cold War* (1998).

Research in ethnochoreology is reported in several publications. Academic research on folkloristics, the study of folklore and its associated genres, is published in *Journal of American Folklore* (quarterly) and *Journal of Folklore Research* (3/yr.). The International Council for Traditional Music includes dance research in the annual *Yearbook for Traditional Music* (which was established as the *Journal of the International Folk Music Council*). Other academic journals that sometimes include articles about folk dance include *Dance Research Journal* (semiannual) and *Ethnomusicology* (3/yr.).

*The JVC Video Anthology of World Music and Dance* (1990), produced by Ichikawa Katsumori and directed by Nakagawa Kunihiko, is a collection of 30 VHS tapes and 9 books that documents hundreds of dances from around the world; it has also been recorded on DVD in 30 discs (2005).

# BALLROOM DANCE

Elizabeth Aldrich, *From the Ballroom to Hell: Grace and Folly in Nineteenth-Century Dance* (1991), not only provides excerpts and illustrations from 19th-century dance manuals and periodicals but also offers a valuable annotated bibliography of dance content in a wide range of 19th-century publications. Linda Tomko, *Dancing Class: Gender, Ethnicity and Social Divides in American Dance, 1890–1920* (1999), examines social and ballroom dance during the period of great change at the turn of the 20th century. Julie Malnig, *Dancing till Dawn: A Century of Exhibition Ballroom Dance* (1992), is a pioneering work on 20th-century exhibition ballroom dance as seen from a feminist perspective. Important collections of essays on ballroom and other forms of social dance include Julie Malnig (ed.), *Ballroom, Boogie, Shimmy Sham, Shake: A Social and Popular Dance Reader* (2009); and Suzanna Sloat (ed.), *Caribbean Dance from Abakuá to Zouk* (2002).

## TAP DANCE

Marshall Stearns and Jean Stearns, *Jazz Dance: The Story of American Vernacular Dance* (1968; reissued with a new foreword and afterword, 1994), is a history of popular dance in the United States; Rusty E. Frank, TAP!: *The Greatest Tap Dance Stars and Their Stories, 1900–1955*, rev. ed. (1994), provides interviews with a number of influential tap dancers; and Mark Knowles, *Tap Roots: The Early History of Tap Dancing* (2002), is a study of the many dance styles that influenced the development of tap.

## JAZZ DANCE

The history of jazz dance is treated in Marshall Stearns and Jean Stearns, *Jazz Dance* (1968, reissued 1994); and in Gus Giordano, *Anthology of American Jazz Dance* (1975), which also includes a graded system of jazz dance, a dictionary of terms, and information on recognized teachers and choreographers.

# HIP-HOP AND BREAK DANCING

David Toop, *Rap Attack 3: African Rap to Global Hip Hop* (1999), is probably the book most successful at revealing hip-hop's debts to earlier forms of African American popular music. In answer to the question of whether hip-hop lyrics are a form of poetry, Lawrence A. Stanley (ed.), *Rap: The Lyrics* (1992), allows readers to make up their own minds by presenting the writings of hip-hop's greatest lyricists. Tricia Rose, *Black Noise: Rap Music and Black Culture in Contemporary America* (1994), argues that technology, urban sociology, race politics, and feminism have intersected in hip-hop to foment a hotbed of postmodern artistry and controversy. Nelson George, *Hip Hop America* (1998), presents a serious fan's view of the long road hip-hop took from street fests to mainstream market profitability and semirespectability. Havelock Nelson and Michael A. Gonzales, *Bring the Noise: A Guide to Rap Music and Hip-Hop*

*Culture* (1991), is a detailed introduction to the history of rap and a guide to the best recordings. Alan Light (ed.), *The Vibe History of Hip Hop* (1999), explores the full scope of hip-hop's origins and expansion with contributions from more than 50 writers; Jeff Chang, *Can't Stop, Won't Stop: A History of the Hip-Hop Generation* (2005), examines the sociocultural and musical history of the genre; Murray Forman and Mark Anthony Neal (eds.), *That's the Joint!: The Hip-Hop Studies Reader* (2004), is a wide-ranging anthology of writings from both the academic and popular press; Sacha Jenkins, Elliott Wilson, Chairman Mao, Gabriel Alvarez, and Brent Rollins, *Ego Trip's Book of Rap Lists* (1999), is humorous and opinionated but dense with information and true to the spirit of the culture. For the origin and development of break dancing, see Gerald D. Jaynes, *Encyclopedia of African American Society* (2005).

# WESTERN DANCE

Curt Sachs, *A World History of the Dance* (1937, reprinted 1965; originally published in German, 1933), the most comprehensive, systematic, and factual history of dance in all its epochs and forms, with special emphasis on its earliest beginnings and close attention to dance accompaniment; W. F. Raffé, *Dictionary of the Dance* (1965, reissued 1975), includes detailed descriptions of the particular dances, their background, and history; Anatole Chujoy and P. W. Manchester (eds.), *The Dance Encyclopedia*, rev. ed. (1967), is a collection of articles on all forms of dancing—particularly detailed in its coverage of ballet, including entries on specific productions, artistic biographies, and histories of ballet in various countries; Horst Koegler, *The Concise Oxford Dictionary of Ballet*, 2nd ed. (1982), is a comprehensive reference work; Lincoln Kirstein, *Dance: A Short History of Classic Theatrical Dancing* (1935, reprinted 1970), is a very thorough book on the preballetic forms of dance as well as classic theatrical dance; Walter Sorell, *The Dance Through the Ages* (1967), is a general, readable survey of the worldwide dance scene from prehistoric times through today, with superb pictures of ancient and modern dance; A. H. Franks, *Social Dance: A Short History* (1963), is the first attempt at relating the origins and developments of the most important social dance forms to their social environment; Frances Rust, *Dance in Society* (1969), a study giving documentary evidence of the social dances and their relationships to the changing structures of society, with emphasis on the English scene and the teenage explosion in dance during the 1960s.

# INDEX